THE NEW FOLGER LIBRARY SHAKESPEARE

Designed to make Shakespeare's great plays available to all readers, the New Folger Library edition of Shakespeare's plays provides accurate texts in modern spelling and punctuation, as well as scene-by-scene action summaries, full explanatory notes, many pictures clarifying Shakespeare's language, and notes recording all significant departures from the early printed versions. Each play is prefaced by a brief introduction, by a guide to reading Shakespeare's language, and by accounts of his life and theater. Each play is followed by an annotated list of further readings and by a "Modern Perspective" written by an expert on that particular play.

Barbara A. Mowat is Director of Academic Programs at the Folger Shakespeare Library, Executive Editor of *Shakespeare Quarterly,* Chair of the Folger Institute, and author of *The Dramaturgy of Shakespeare's Romances* and of essays on Shakespeare's plays and on the editing of the plays.

Paul Werstine is Professor of English at the Graduate School and at King's University College at the University of Western Ontario. He is general editor of the New Variorum Shakespeare and author of many papers and articles on the printing and editing of Shakespeare's plays.

The Folger Shakespeare Library

The Folger Shakespeare Library in Washington, D.C., a privately funded research library dedicated to Shakespeare and the civilization of early modern Europe, was founded in 1932 by Henry Clay and Emily Jordan Folger. In addition to its role as the world's preeminent Shakespeare collection and its emergence as a leading center for Renaissance studies, the Folger Library offers a wide array of cultural and educational programs and services for the general public.

EDITORS

BARBARA A. MOWAT
Director of Academic Programs
Folger Shakespeare Library

PAUL WERSTINE
Professor of English
King's University College at the University of
Western Ontario, Canada

FOLGER SHAKESPEARE LIBRARY

Pericles,

Prince of Tyre

By

WILLIAM SHAKESPEARE

EDITED BY BARBARA A. MOWAT
AND PAUL WERSTINE

WASHINGTON SQUARE PRESS

NEW YORK   LONDON   TORONTO   SYDNEY

A WASHINGTON SQUARE PRESS *Original* Publication

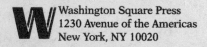

Washington Square Press
1230 Avenue of the Americas
New York, NY 10020

Copyright © 2005 by The Folger Shakespeare Library

ISBN-13: 978-0-7432-7329-9
ISBN-10:   0-7432-7329-X

Washington Square Press New Folger Edition October 2005

10 9 8 7 6 5 4 3 2 1

WASHINGTON SQUARE PRESS and colophon are registered trademarks of Simon & Schuster, Inc.

Manufactured in the United States of America

For information regarding special discounts for bulk purchases, please contact Simon & Schuster Special Sales at 1-800-456-6798 or business@simonandschuster.com.

From the Director of the Library

Shakespeare has never been more alive as author and playwright than he is today, with productions being staged all over the world, new film versions appearing on screen every year, and millions of students in classrooms at all levels absorbed in the human drama and verbal richness of his works.

The New Folger Library Shakespeare editions welcome the interested reader with newly edited texts, commentary in a friendly facing-page format, and illustrations, drawn from the Folger archives, that wonderfully illuminate references and images in the plays. A synopsis of every scene makes the action clear.

In these editions, students, teachers, actors, and thousands of other readers will find the best of modern textual scholarship, along with up-to-date critical essays, written especially for these volumes, that offer original and often surprising interpretations of Shakespeare's characters, action, and language.

I thank editors Barbara Mowat and Paul Werstine for undertaking this ambitious project, which is nothing less than an entirely new look at the texts from the earliest printed versions. Lovers of Shakespeare everywhere must be grateful for the breadth of their learning, the liveliness of their imaginations, and the scholarly rigor that they bring to the challenge of re-editing the plays.

Gail Kern Paster, Director
The Folger Shakespeare Library

Contents

Contents

Editors' Preface

In recent years, ways of dealing with Shakespeare's texts and with the interpretation of his plays have been undergoing significant change. This edition, while retaining many of the features that have always made the Folger Shakespeare so attractive to the general reader, at the same time reflects these current ways of thinking about Shakespeare. For example, modern readers, actors, and teachers have become interested in the differences between, on the one hand, the early forms in which Shakespeare's plays were first published and, on the other hand, the forms in which editors through the centuries have presented them. In response to this interest, we have based our edition on what we consider the best early printed version of a particular play (explaining our rationale in a section called "An Introduction to This Text") and have marked our changes in the text—unobtrusively, we hope, but in such a way that the curious reader can be aware that a change has been made and can consult the "Textual Notes" to discover what appeared in the early printed version.

Current ways of looking at the plays are reflected in our brief prefaces, in many of the commentary notes, in the annotated lists of "Further Reading," and especially in each play's "Modern Perspective," an essay written by an outstanding scholar who brings to the reader his or her fresh assessment of the play in the light of today's interests and concerns.

As in the Folger Library General Reader's Shakespeare, which this edition replaces, we include explanatory notes designed to help make Shakespeare's language clearer to a modern reader, and we place the notes on the page facing the text that they explain. We also follow the earlier edition in including illustrations—of objects, of clothing, of mythological figures—from books and manuscripts in the Folger Library collection. We provide fresh accounts of the life of Shakespeare, of the publishing of his plays, and of the theaters in which his plays were performed, as well as an introduction to the text itself. We also include a section called "Reading Shakespeare's Language," in which we try to help readers learn to "break the code" of Elizabethan poetic language.

For each section of each volume, we are indebted to a host of generous experts and fellow scholars. The "Reading Shakespeare's Language" sections, for example, could not have been written had not Arthur King, of Brigham Young University, and Randall Robinson, author of *Unlocking Shakespeare's Language,* led the way in untangling Shakespearean language puzzles and shared their insights and methodologies generously with us. "Shakespeare's Life" profited by the careful reading given it by the late S. Schoenbaum; "Shakespeare's Theater" was read and strengthened by Andrew Gurr, John Astington, and William Ingram; and "The Publication of Shakespeare's Plays" is indebted to the comments of Peter W. M. Blayney. We, as editors, take sole responsibility for any errors in our editions.

We are grateful to the authors of the "Modern Perspectives"; to the Huntington and Newberry Libraries for fellowship support; to King's University College for the grants it has provided to Paul Werstine; to the Social Sciences and Humanities Research Council of Canada, which provided him with a Research Time Stipend for 1990–91; to R. J. Shroyer of the University of Western Ontario for essential computer support; to the Folger Institute's Center for Shakespeare Studies for its sponsorship of a workshop on "Shakespeare's Texts for Students and Teachers" (funded by the National Endowment for the Humanities and led by Richard Knowles of the University of Wisconsin), a workshop from which we learned an enormous amount about what is wanted by college and high-school teachers of Shakespeare today; to Alice Falk for her expert copyediting; and especially to Stephen Llano, our production editor at Washington Square Press, whose expertise and attention to detail are essential to this project. Among the texts we consulted, we found Suzanne Gossett's Arden *Pericles* (2004) particularly helpful.

Our biggest debt is to the Folger Shakespeare Library—to Gail Kern Paster, Director of the Library, whose interest and support are unfailing, and to Werner Gundersheimer, the Library's Director from 1984 to 2002, who made possible our edition; to Deborah Curren-Aquino, who provides extensive editorial and production support; to Jean Miller, the Library's former Art Curator, who combs the Library holdings for illustrations, and to Julie Ainsworth, Head of the Photography Department, who carefully photographs them; to Peggy O'Brien, former Director of Education at the Folger and now Senior Vice President, Educational Programming and Services, at the Corporation for Public Broadcasting, who gave us expert advice about the needs being expressed by Shakespeare teachers and students (and to Martha Christian and other "master teachers" who used our texts in manuscript in their classrooms); to Allan Shnerson and Mary Bloodworth for their expert computer support; to the staff of the Academic Programs Division, especially Solvei Robertson (whose help is crucial), Mary Tonkinson, Kathleen Lynch, Carol Brobeck, Liz Pohland, Owen Williams, and Virginia Millington; and, finally, to the generously supportive staff of the Library's Reading Room.

Barbara A. Mowat and Paul Werstine

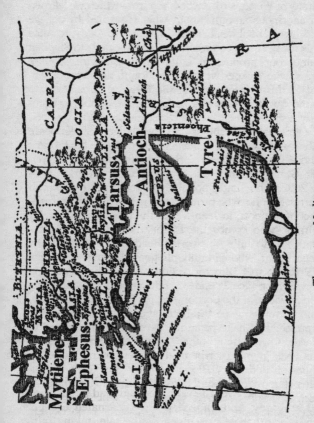

The eastern Mediterranean.

From Herman Moll. . . . *Maps of the geography of the ancients . . . .* (1726).

Shakespeare's *Pericles*

Pericles tells the story of a prince who, as a young man in search of a wife, finds a gorgeous princess; he risks his life to win her, but discovers that she is in an incestuous relationship with her father; the discovery not only disgusts him but also puts him in mortal danger from her father, and he flees. This is only the beginning of Pericles' travails. After many adventures, including a near-fatal shipwreck, he meets another princess with whom he falls in love; this time the love leads to marriage. He and his pregnant wife set out for his kingdom, but in a tempest at sea his wife dies in giving birth to their daughter. The series of adventures continues, following the narrative pattern of "and then ... and then ... and then ..." through one disaster after another until the daughter, now grown up, pulls her grief-stricken father out of the depths of his despair and the play moves toward its gloriously happy ending.

This play, patterned as a sequence of adventures and misadventures, is clearly not typical of Shakespearean drama, and the opening lines of the play prepare us for its strangeness. A speaker, using archaic language, introduces himself as the medieval poet John Gower come back from the grave to tell us a story from long ago, one recited over the centuries and read by many a lord and lady. And, indeed, this reincarnated Gower does proceed to tell us much of the tale, taking our imaginations from one spot to another in the eastern Mediterranean, introducing scenes of dialogue and action, pronouncing judgment on characters good and bad, and sometimes filling in extensive gaps in the story. Woven into and around Gower's narration are dumb shows (scenes of action without speech) and spectacular dramatized scenes—scenes of starving kings and citizens, of shipwrecks and storms at sea, of courtly banquets and martial dancing, of brothel life and supernatural visions—but it is Gower who holds the story together and guides us through time and space. The play's structure, then, is like a narrative that periodically breaks into dramatic life.

Such an unusual way of shaping a drama is not only fascinating but also fitting, since *Pericles* tells the kind of romance tale that one associates more with "once-upon-a-time" storytelling than with theater. The play's story is a version of one of several ancient popular tales about a hero who, after great trials and long journeys, successfully establishes a family, only to lose both wife and children; time then passes, his fortunes finally change, and, in a near-miraculous fashion, he recovers both the children and the wife. That Shakespeare had been interested in this kind of tale from the very beginning of his career is shown in the frame story of family separation and reunion that surrounds the one-day action of the very early *The Comedy of Errors*, and we find versions of this same romance plot in *Twelfth Night*, *The Winter's Tale*, and *Cymbeline* as well. What sets *Pericles* apart from these other romance-based plays is its openly narrative structure and the deliberately archaic verse in which Gower-as-Chorus speaks.

Because *Pericles* is so unusual in its structure, because it was not included in the Folio of 1623, and because much of the text in which it survives is so problematic, this play remains on the periphery of Shakespeare's work, with some scholars in the past arguing that it is not by Shakespeare, and many scholars today insisting that another playwright wrote much of it. Yet *Pericles* shares multiple features with many of Shakespeare's plays, it tells the kind of story that Shakespeare turned to often in his career, and it presents the story in a highly experimental manner—a characteristic of the plays that, like *Pericles*, Shakespeare wrote late in his career. Whatever the scholarly doubts about the authorship of the play, a good production shows that it has the power and the strong emotional effect that one associates most of all with Shakespeare.

After you have read the play, we invite you to turn to the essay printed after it, *"Pericles:* A Modern Perspective," written by Professor Margaret Jane Kidnie of the University of Western Ontario.

Reading Shakespeare's Language: *Pericles*

For many people today, reading Shakespeare's language can be a problem—but it is a problem that can be solved. Those who have studied Latin (or even French or German or Spanish), and those who are used to reading poetry, will have little difficulty understanding the language of Shakespeare's poetic drama. Others, though, need to develop the skills of untangling unusual sentence structures and of recognizing and understanding poetic compressions, omissions, and wordplay. And even those skilled in reading unusual sentence structures may have occasional trouble with Shakespeare's words. Four hundred years of "static" intervene between his speaking and our hearing. Most of his immense vocabulary is still in use, but a few of his words are not, and, worse, some of his words now have meanings quite different from those they had in the sixteenth and seventeenth centuries. In the theater, most of these difficulties are solved for us by actors who study the language and articulate it for us so that the essential meaning is heard—or, when combined with stage action, is at least *felt*. When reading on one's own, one must do what each actor does: go over the lines (often with a dictionary close at hand) until the puzzles are solved and the lines yield up their poetry and the characters speak in words and phrases that are, suddenly, rewarding and wonderfully memorable.

Shakespeare's Words

As you begin to read the opening scenes of a play by Shakespeare, you may notice occasional unfamiliar words. Some are unfamiliar simply because we no longer use them. In the opening scenes of *Pericles*, for example, you will find the words *wight* (i.e., creature), *erst* (i.e., not long ago), *physic* (i.e., medicine), and *ostent* (i.e., display). Words of this kind are explained in notes to the text and will become familiar the more of Shakespeare's plays you read.

In *Pericles*, as in all of Shakespeare's writing, more problematic are the words that we still use but that we use with a different meaning. For instance, in the opening scenes of *Pericles* the word *targets* has the meaning of "shields," *partakes* is used where we would say "imparts," *convince* is used where we would say "confute," and *curious* where we would say "exquisite." Such words will be explained in the notes to the text, but they, too, will become familiar as you continue to read Shakespeare's language.

Some words are strange not because of the "static" introduced by changes in language over the past centuries but because these are words that Shakespeare is using to build a dramatic world that has its own space, time, and history. In *Pericles*, Shakespeare presents the narrator Gower as reappearing from the long past by having him speak not only in an old-fashioned verse form but also in words that would seem archaic to Shakespeare's audience. Gower's narrations include such words as "iwis," "speken," "ne aught escapend," and "yslackèd," words that were either used by John Gower in his fourteenth-century telling of the Pericles story or that sound like his language. When we move from Gower's narrations to scenes of dialogue and action, the play's language places it in a generally aristocratic world that is vaguely Greco-Roman; the opening scene, for example, includes references to such ancient Roman gods as "Jove," "Lucina," and "Cupid," as well as to the mythological "Graces" and the "Hesperides" and their "dragon." These Greco-Roman allusions are Shakespeare's contributions to the story he inherited from Gower and Twine, both of whose supernatural references are strictly Christian. (For Gower and Twine, see the Appendix.) The scene also uses language from the world of chivalry, turning Pericles' attempt to solve a riddle into a knightly "adventure" with death as the "hazard": Pericles, facing his dangerous "task," is to be " 'sayed" (i.e., essayed, tested in combat), and, in the manner of a knight preparing to do battle, "like a bold champion [he] assume[s] the lists." Like the language of Greco-Roman mythology, this language of chivalry is Shakespeare's contribution to the story—a contribution that is literalized in the third act of the play, where *Pericles* introduces chivalric shields and armor in place of the naked wrestling and tennis in Gower and Twine and substitutes a tournament and a dance of knights in armor for the competition by way of written accounts of ancestry and possessions, the version found in Gower and Twine.

The language that opens the first scene of Act 2, when the action shifts to the coast of Pentapolis, creates a world very different from the previous aristocratic worlds of Antioch, Tyre, and Tarsus. The fishermen who find the shipwrecked Pericles are given the language of lower-class Elizabethans: they use such expressions as "Marry," "welladay," "Bots on 't," and "Come away, or I'll fetch thee with a wanion," and they allude to such Elizabethan commonplaces as "the whole parish—church, steeple, bells and all," to the parish "beadle," the "belfry," and "puddings and flapjacks." A comparable language set constructs the world of the brothel in Act 4, where the Bawd and her accomplices use such expressions as "Marry, whip the gosling!" and "Come your ways," and where the conversation is about "sodden" "creatures" (prostitutes waterlogged from treatment for venereal disease) who have "pooped" the "gallants" of Mytilene until they cower "i' the hams" from syphilis.

Shakespeare's Sentences

In an English sentence, meaning is quite dependent on the place given each word. "The dog bit the boy" and "The boy bit the dog" mean very different things, even though the individual words are the same. Because English places such importance on the positions of words in sentences, on the way words are arranged, unusual arrangements can puzzle a reader. Shakespeare frequently shifts his sentences away from "normal" English arrangements—often to create the rhythm he seeks, sometimes to use a line's poetic rhythm to emphasize a particular word, sometimes to give a character his or her own speech patterns or to allow the character to speak in a special way. When we attend a good performance of the play, the actors will have worked out the sentence structures and will articulate the sentences so that the meaning is clear. (Sometimes the language of *Pericles* steadfastly resists any clear meaning. But the actors will, nonetheless, clarify it as far as the words and sentence structure allow.) In reading for ourselves, we should do as the actor does. That is, when we become puzzled by a character's speech, we should check to see if words are being presented in an unusual sequence.

Shakespeare often, for example, places the object before the verb (i.e., instead of "I hit him," we might find "I him hit"). In *Pericles*, Antiochus's "Nature this dowry gave" (1.1.10) is an example of an object-verb inversion, as is Pericles' "the womb that their first being bred" (1.1.112). (The "normal" order would be "Nature gave this dowry" and "the womb that bred their first being.") Inversions are not the only unusual sentence structures in Shakespeare's language. Often in his sentences words that would normally appear together are separated from each other. Again, this is frequently done to create a particular rhythm or to foreground particular words or phrases. Take, for example, Antiochus's warning speech to Pericles:

Yon sometimes famous *princes*, like thyself,
Drawn by report, advent'rous by desire,
Tell thee with speechless tongues and semblance pale
That, without covering save yon field of stars,
Here they stand martyrs slain in Cupid's wars . . .
                                        (1.1.35–39)

Here, a series of phrases that describe the "princes" ("like thyself," "Drawn by report," "advent'rous by desire") separate the subject ("princes") from the verb and its indirect object ("Tell thee"); the phrase "with speechless tongues and semblance pale" separates the verb from its direct object ("That . . . Here they stand"), just as the phrase "without covering save yon field of stars" separates the conjunctive particle ("That") from the clause it introduces. These longer phrases, placed as they are as "interrupters," foreground the horror with which Pericles is being threatened, the horror of being reduced to a severed head on a pole or gate.

Pericles' speech in 1.2 uses interruptions in a similar way:

> The great *Antiochus*,
> 'Gainst whom I am too little to contend,
> Since he's so great can make his will his act,
> *Will think* me speaking though I swear to silence . . .
>
> (19–22)

Here, the subject "Antiochus" is separated from the verb "Will think" by two clauses that are not logically connected to the subject and verb. In other words, they do not explain why Antiochus will think that Pericles is speaking against him. Instead, they explain why Pericles is afraid of Antiochus's misunderstanding of his behavior: Antiochus is far more powerful than Pericles, so great, in fact, that he can do whatever he likes. The placement of this recognition as an interruption instead of in a sentence of its own suggests the panic that dominates Pericles' thoughts, exemplifying "the passions of the mind" that Pericles meditates upon. In order to create for yourself sentences that seem more like the English of everyday speech, you may wish to rearrange the words, putting together the word clusters ("Yon princes tell thee that here they stand"; "Antiochus will think"). You will usually find that the sentence will gain in clarity but will lose its rhythm or shift its emphasis.

Sometimes, rather than separating basic sentence elements, Shakespeare simply holds them back, delaying them until other material to which he wants to give greater emphasis has been presented. Shakespeare uses a version of this construction in *Pericles* in Helicanus's speech to the impatient lords of Tyre:

> If further yet you will be satisfied
> Why, as it were, unlicensed of your loves
> He would depart, *I'll give some light unto you.*
>
> (1.3.16–18)

In the previous speech, Helicanus had said that the lords should not question him about Pericles' departure, since the sealed commission Pericles has left behind conferring his authority on Helicanus is ample testimony to the prince's absence. In the present speech, he nevertheless presents an answer to their questions, prefacing his concession to their demands ("I'll give some light unto you") with an ambiguous locution that perhaps blames the lords for wishing for yet more of an explanation ("if further yet you will be satisfied"); and, in the oddly phrased "unlicensed of your loves" (i.e., without permission from you, his loving subjects), he perhaps chastises them for an improper sense of their own importance. (Helicanus's prefatory "if" clause can instead be interpreted by the actor not as accusatory but as a simple acknowledgment that the lords have a right to know why Pericles left without explaining his departure.)

Finally, in many of Shakespeare's plays, sentences are sometimes complicated not because of unusual

structures or interruptions but because Shakespeare,
through ellipsis, omits words and parts of words that
English sentences normally require. (In conversation,
we, too, often omit words. We say, "Heard from him
yet?" and our hearer supplies the missing "Have
you.") Frequent reading of Shakespeare—and of other
poets—trains us to supply such missing words. *Pericles*, like Shakespeare's other late plays, uses omissions frequently. Sometimes the ellipses are easily
filled in by the auditor or reader. When Pericles says,
for example,

> *Who has a book* of all that monarchs do,
> He's more secure to keep it shut than shown.
> For vice repeated is like the wand'ring wind,
> *Blows dust* in others' eyes to spread itself[,]
>
> (1.1.97–100)

it is clear that "Who has a book" is to be understood to
read "[He] who has a book," and "wind, / Blows dust," to
read "wind [that] blows dust." However, Pericles'
description of Antiochus's daughter is more challenging:

> See where she comes, appareled like the spring,
> *Graces her subjects*, and *her thoughts the king*
> Of *every virtue gives* renown to men!
>
> (1.1.13–15)

"Every virtue gives" is clearly to be read as "every
virtue [that] gives," but it is more difficult to expand
the ellipses in "Graces her subjects" ("[With the]
Graces [as] her subjects"? "[The] Graces [are] her subjects"?) and to clarify "her thoughts the king" ("[with]
her thoughts [as] the king"? "her thoughts [are] the
king"?). Whether it is easy or difficult to fill in the

ellipses, doing so—making Pericles say "[he] who has a book," or "every virtue [that] gives renown"—destroys not only the rhythm of the verse but also the play's characteristic highly cryptic style.

Shakespearean Wordplay

Shakespeare plays with language so often and so variously that entire books are written on the topic. Here we will mention only two kinds of wordplay, puns and metaphors. A pun is a play on words that sound the same but have different meanings or on a single word with more than one meaning. In *Pericles*, puns usually play on the multiple meanings of a single word. When, for example, Pericles says, in his farewell to Helicanus in 1.2, "in our orbs we'll live so round and safe" (130), he uses the word *orbs* to mean "spheres of action," but the word also refers to the circular paths or spheres in which, according to Ptolemaic cosmology, planets circled the earth. This double meaning leads to the pun on *round* (in "we'll live so round"), where *round* means "honestly, straightforwardly," but with wordplay on the circularity of the orb. Again, when, in 2.1, Pericles says that the sea has cast him on the fishermen's coast, the Second Fisherman replies, "What a drunken knave was the sea to cast thee in our way!" (59–60), punning on *cast* as (1) throw and (2) vomit. In 2.3, King Simonides, who seems to love bawdy puns, tells the knights that women "love men in arms as well as beds" (102), punning on *in arms* as (1) dressed in armor and (2) in the women's arms. A few lines later, he encourages Pericles to dance by saying "I have heard you knights of Tyre / Are excellent in making ladies trip" (106–7); here he puns on *trip* as (1) dance nimbly and (2) fall (i.e., sin).

At two moments in *Pericles*, puns are used in particularly interesting ways. The first is near the end of the Chorus that introduces Act 4, where Gower says to the audience

> I carry wingèd Time
> Post on the lame feet of my rhyme,
> Which never could I so convey
> Unless your thoughts went on my way.
>
> (4 Chor. 47–50)

By punning on *lame* (as "crippled" and "metrically defective"), on *feet* (as his own "feet" and as "divisions of a verse"), and on *convey* (as "transport" and "communicate"), Gower is able to defend his moving the action forward by many years by wittily claiming that his verse has been heroically carrying the proverbial figure of "wingèd Time." The second, and more profound, instance of interesting punning is found in Act 5, when Pericles refers to Marina as "Thou that beget'st him that did thee beget" (5.1.229), playing on *beget* as "to call into being" and "to father." This line, arguably the most powerful in *Pericles*, shows that puns need not be merely trivial or amusing.

A metaphor is a play on words in which one object or idea is expressed as if it were something else, something with which it shares common features. When Pericles first sees the daughter of King Antiochus, he uses metaphor to capture her beauty and desirability: "You gods . . . / That have inflamed desire in my breast / To taste the fruit of yon celestial tree / Or die in th' adventure, be my helps" (1.1.20–23). In his language, the princess is a "celestial tree" bearing delicious "fruit" of which he would "taste." In Antiochus's speech that follows, the metaphor continues, but with significant alterations: "Before thee stands this fair Hesperides, / With golden fruit, but dangerous to be touched; / For death-like dragons here affright thee hard" (28–30). Transforming the metaphor by replacing the celestial tree with the mythological garden of the Hesperides, Antiochus retains the attractiveness of the fruit while reminding Pericles that it is a source of mortal danger. (In mythology, the golden apples of the Hesperides were guarded not only by nymphs but also by a dragon that never slept; overcoming it was one of the labors of Hercules.) Antiochus uses metaphor again when he says, in the same speech, that the princes who have died seeking his daughter's hand are "martyrs slain in Cupid's wars" (39). The princes, in other words, have "died for love," but his metaphor represents them as dead bodies strewn on a battleground, dead as a consequence of fighting for Cupid. While the word *martyr* could signify one dying as a consequence of his devotion to any belief, it inevitably carries some of its earliest and continuing religious meaning of one who willingly dies rather than renounce his Christian faith; thus Antiochus's metaphor implicitly accuses the dead princes of choosing religious martyrdom, refusing to renounce their faith (in Cupid) and going willfully to their deaths.

Pericles is so filled with metaphoric language that almost every speech could provide an example, but one specific metaphor—that in which a person's face or a person's history becomes a book for another to read—is worth singling out for comment. Pericles introduces the figure when he says of Antiochus's daughter: "Her face the book of praises, where is read / Nothing but curious [i.e., exquisite] pleasures" (1.1.16–17). The metaphor, here expressed quite simply, is given a more elaborate form by King Simonides in his courtly, adulatory refusal to commend the knights celebrating Thaisa's birthday:

> To place upon the volume of your deeds,
> As in a title page, your worth in arms
> Were more than you expect or more than 's fit,
> Since every worth in show commends itself.
>
> (2.3.3–6)

Here, the knights' martial deeds are imagined as a book on which Simonides declines to place a flattering title page, since the content of the book "commends itself." Book-related metaphors call attention to themselves in *Pericles*, in part because Gower as Chorus repeatedly cites the "authors" whose books his story retells and because John Gower himself was closely linked in the imaginations of Shakespeare's day with the book as artifact: his tomb in the church of St. Mary Overie (now known as Southwark Cathedral or St. Saviors, Southwark) is ornamented with a stone image of the poet with its head pillowed on a stone replica of a pile of books—Gower's three important folio works. Because metaphors are so central to the language of *Pericles*, the actor, the reader, and the spectator must be willing to exert an unusual amount of energy in responding to this play.

Implied Stage Action

Finally, in reading Shakespeare's plays we should always remember that what we are reading is a performance script. The dialogue is written to be spoken by actors who, at the same time, are moving, gesturing, picking up objects, weeping, shaking their fists. Some stage action is described in what are called "stage directions"; some is suggested within the dialogue itself. We must learn to be alert to such signals as we stage the play in our imaginations. When Antiochus says to Thaliard "Here's poison, and here's gold. / We hate the Prince / Of Tyre, and thou must kill him. . . . / . . . Say, is it done?" and Thaliard replies "My lord, 'tis done" (1.1.162–67), it is clear that Antiochus, when saying "Here's poison, and here's gold," has actually handed Thaliard the poison and the money. Again, when Helicanus, in chastising Pericles, says "Prince, pardon me, or strike me, if you please. / I cannot be much lower than my knees," and, a few lines later, Pericles says to him "Rise, prithee rise" (1.2.49–50, 64), it is clear that Helicanus's "I cannot be much lower than my knees" signals that he has kneeled or is at that moment kneeling.

Occasionally in *Pericles*, signals to the reader are not quite so clear. When in the first scene, for example, Antiochus says "Prince Pericles, touch not, upon thy life," Pericles has doubtless made some kind of gesture that Antiochus misinterprets, though it is difficult to imagine just what that might be. (Pericles has said clearly in an aside that he has no desire to touch in any loving way the incestuous daughter.) Another example occurs later in the play, where, even with early printed stage directions, the stage action remains ambiguous. King Simonides demands a "soldiers' dance," telling the knights that they should dance in their armor and to loud music, since ladies "love men in arms as well as beds." The Quarto stage direction then reads *"They dance."* Neither Simonides' language nor the stage direction makes clear whether only the knights in armor dance or whether they dance with the ladies. The king later insists that Pericles dance with Thaisa. Again, the Quarto stage direction reads *"They dance."* And again editors and directors are divided about whether this is a dance of knights and ladies generally or only of Pericles and Thaisa. It is thus possible to stage this scene in several ways, both in the theater and in one's imagination. Learning to read the language of stage action repays one many times over when one reaches a crucial scene like 5.3, in which implied stage action vitally affects our response to the play.

It is immensely rewarding to work carefully with Shakespeare's language—with the words, the sentences, the wordplay, and the implied stage action—as readers for the past four centuries have discovered. It may be more pleasurable to attend a good performance of a play—though not everyone has thought so. But the joy of being able to stage one of Shakespeare's plays in one's imagination, to return to passages that continue to yield further meanings (or further questions) the more one reads them—these are pleasures that, for many, rival (or at least augment) those of the performed text, and certainly make it worth considerable effort to "break the code" of Elizabethan poetic drama and let free the remarkable language that makes up a Shakespeare text.

Shakespeare's Life

Surviving documents that give us glimpses into the life of William Shakespeare show us a playwright, poet, and actor who grew up in the market town of Stratford-upon-Avon, spent his professional life in London, and returned to Stratford a wealthy landowner. He was born in April 1564, died in April 1616, and is buried inside the chancel of Holy Trinity Church in Stratford.

We wish we could know more about the life of the world's greatest dramatist. His plays and poems are testaments to his wide reading—especially to his knowledge of Virgil, Ovid, Plutarch, Holinshed's *Chronicles*, and the Bible—and to his mastery of the English language, but we can only speculate about his education. We know that the King's New School in Stratford-upon-Avon was considered excellent. The school was one of the English "grammar schools" established to educate young men, primarily in Latin grammar and literature. As in other schools of the time, students began their studies at the age of four or five in the attached "petty school," and there learned to read and write in English, studying primarily the catechism from the Book of Common Prayer. After two years in the petty school, students entered the lower form (grade) of the grammar school, where they began the serious study of Latin grammar and Latin texts that would occupy most of the remainder of their school days. (Several Latin texts that Shakespeare used repeatedly in writing his plays and poems were texts that schoolboys memorized and recited.) Latin comedies were introduced early in the lower form; in the upper form, which the boys entered at age ten or eleven, students wrote their own Latin orations and declamations, studied Latin historians and rhetoricians, and began the study of Greek using the Greek New Testament.

Since the records of the Stratford "grammar school" do not survive, we cannot prove that William Shakespeare attended the school; however, every indication (his father's position as an alderman and bailiff of Stratford, the playwright's own knowledge of the Latin classics, scenes in the plays that recall grammar-school experiences—for example, *The Merry Wives of Windsor*, 4.1) suggests that he did. We also lack generally accepted documentation about Shakespeare's life after his schooling ended and his professional life in

London began. His marriage in 1582 (at age eighteen) to Anne Hathaway and the subsequent births of his daughter Susanna (1583) and the twins Judith and Hamnet (1585) are recorded, but how he supported himself and where he lived are not known. Nor do we know when and why he left Stratford for the London theatrical world, nor how he rose to be the important figure in that world that he had become by the early 1590s.

We do know that by 1592 he had achieved some prominence in London as both an actor and a playwright. In that year was published a book by the playwright Robert Greene attacking an actor who had the audacity to write blank-verse drama and who was "in his own conceit [i.e., opinion] the only Shake-scene in a country." Since Greene's attack includes a parody of a line from one of Shakespeare's early plays, there is little doubt that it is Shakespeare to whom he refers, a "Shake-scene" who had aroused Greene's fury by successfully competing with university-educated dramatists like Greene himself. It was in 1593 that Shakespeare became a published poet. In that year he published his long narrative poem *Venus and Adonis;* in 1594, he followed it with *The Rape of Lucrece.* Both poems were dedicated to the young earl of Southampton (Henry Wriothesley), who may have become Shakespeare's patron.

It seems no coincidence that Shakespeare wrote these narrative poems at a time when the theaters were closed because of the plague, a contagious epidemic disease that devastated the population of London. When the theaters reopened in 1594, Shakespeare apparently resumed his double career of actor and playwright and began his long (and seemingly profitable) service as an acting-company shareholder. Records for December of 1594 show him to be a leading member of the Lord

Chamberlain's Men. It was this company of actors, later named the King's Men, for whom he would be a principal actor, dramatist, and shareholder for the rest of his career.

So far as we can tell, that career spanned about twenty years. In the 1590s, he wrote his plays on English history as well as several comedies and at least two tragedies (*Titus Andronicus* and *Romeo and Juliet*). These histories, comedies, and tragedies are the plays credited to him in 1598 in a work, *Palladis Tamia,* that in one chapter compares English writers with "Greek, Latin, and Italian Poets." There the author, Francis Meres, claims that Shakespeare is comparable to the Latin dramatists Seneca for tragedy and Plautus for comedy, and calls him "the most excellent in both kinds for the stage." He also names him "Mellifluous and honey-tongued Shakespeare": "I say," writes Meres, "that the Muses would speak with Shakespeare's fine filed phrase, if they would speak English." Since Meres also mentions Shakespeare's "sugared sonnets among his private friends," it is assumed that many of Shakespeare's sonnets (not published until 1609) were also written in the 1590s.

In 1599, Shakespeare's company built a theater for themselves across the river from London, naming it the Globe. The plays that are considered by many to be Shakespeare's major tragedies (*Hamlet, Othello, King Lear,* and *Macbeth*) were written while the company was resident in this theater, as were such comedies as *Twelfth Night* and *Measure for Measure.* Many of Shakespeare's plays were performed at court (both for Queen Elizabeth I and, after her death in 1603, for King James I), some were presented at the Inns of Court (the residences of London's legal societies), and some were doubtless performed in other towns, at the universities, and at great houses when the King's Men went on tour; otherwise, his plays from 1599 to 1608 were, so far as we know, performed only at the Globe. Between 1608 and 1612, Shakespeare wrote several plays—among them *The Winter's Tale* and *The Tempest*—presumably for the company's new indoor Blackfriars theater, though the plays seem to have been performed also at the Globe and at court. Surviving documents describe a performance of *The Winter's Tale* in 1611 at the Globe, for example, and performances of *The Tempest* in 1611 and 1613 at the royal palace of Whitehall.

Shakespeare wrote very little after 1612, the year in which he probably wrote *King Henry VIII*. (It was at a performance of *Henry VIII* in 1613 that the Globe caught fire and burned to the ground.) Sometime between 1610 and 1613 he seems to have returned to live in Stratford-upon-Avon, where he owned a large house and considerable property, and where his wife and his two daughters and their husbands lived. (His son Hamnet had died in 1596.) During his professional years in London, Shakespeare had presumably derived income from the acting company's profits as well as from his own career as an actor, from the sale of his play manuscripts to the acting company, and, after 1599, from his shares as an owner of the Globe. It was presumably that income, carefully invested in land and other property, which made him the wealthy man that surviving documents show him to have become. It is also assumed that William Shakespeare's growing wealth and reputation played some part in inclining the crown, in 1596, to grant John Shakespeare, William's father, the coat of arms that he had so long sought. William Shakespeare died in Stratford on April 23, 1616 (according to the epitaph carved under his bust in Holy Trinity Church) and was buried on April 25. Seven years after his death, his collected plays were published as *Mr. William Shakespeares Comedies, Histories, & Tragedies* (the work now known as the First Folio).

The Globe

A stylized representation of the Globe theater.
From Claes Jansz Visscher, *Londinum florentissima
Britanniae urbs . . .* [c. 1625].

The years in which Shakespeare wrote were among the most exciting in English history. Intellectually, the discovery, translation, and printing of Greek and Roman classics were making available a set of works and worldviews that interacted complexly with Christian texts and beliefs. The result was a questioning, a vital intellectual ferment, that provided energy for the period's amazing dramatic and literary output and that fed directly into Shakespeare's plays. The Ghost in *Hamlet*, for example, is wonderfully complicated in part because he is a figure from Roman tragedy—the spirit of the dead returning to seek revenge—who at the same time inhabits a Christian hell (or purgatory); Hamlet's description of humankind reflects at one moment the Neoplatonic wonderment at mankind ("What a piece of work is a man!") and, at the next, the Christian disparagement of human sinners ("And yet, to me, what is this quintessence of dust?").

As intellectual horizons expanded, so also did geographical and cosmological horizons. New worlds—both North and South America—were explored, and in them were found human beings who lived and worshiped in ways radically different from those of Renaissance Europeans and Englishmen. The universe during these years also seemed to shift and expand. Copernicus had earlier theorized that the earth was not the center of the cosmos but revolved as a planet around the sun. Galileo's telescope, created in 1609, allowed scientists to see that Copernicus had been correct; the universe was not organized with the earth at the center, nor was it so nicely circumscribed as people had, until that time, thought. In terms of expanding horizons, the impact of these discoveries on people's beliefs—religious, scientific, and philosophical—cannot be overstated.

London, too, rapidly expanded and changed during

the years (from the early 1590s to around 1610) that Shakespeare lived there. London—the center of England's government, its economy, its royal court, its overseas trade—was, during these years, becoming an exciting metropolis, drawing to it thousands of new citizens every year. Troubled by overcrowding, by poverty, by recurring epidemics of the plague, London was also a mecca for the wealthy and the aristocratic, and for those who sought advancement at court, or power in government or finance or trade. One hears in Shakespeare's plays the voices of London—the struggles for power, the fear of venereal disease, the language of buying and selling. One hears as well the voices of Stratford-upon-Avon—references to the nearby Forest of Arden, to sheepherding, to small-town gossip, to village fairs and markets. Part of the richness of Shakespeare's work is the influence felt there of the various worlds in which he lived: the world of metropolitan London, the world of small-town and rural England, the world of the theater, and the worlds of craftsmen and shepherds.

That Shakespeare inhabited such worlds we know from surviving London and Stratford documents, as well as from the evidence of the plays and poems themselves. From such records we can sketch the dramatist's life. We know from his works that he was a voracious reader. We know from legal and business documents that he was a multifaceted theater man who became a wealthy landowner. We know a bit about his family life and a fair amount about his legal and financial dealings. Most scholars today depend upon such evidence as they draw their picture of the world's greatest playwright. Such, however, has not always been the case. Until the late eighteenth century, the William Shakespeare who lived in most biographies was the creation of legend and tradition. This was the Shakespeare who was supposedly caught poaching deer at Charlecote, the estate of Sir Thomas Lucy close by Stratford; this was the Shakespeare who fled from Sir Thomas's vengeance and made his way in London by taking care of horses outside a playhouse; this was the Shakespeare who reportedly could barely read but whose natural gifts were extraordinary, whose father was a butcher who allowed his gifted son sometimes to help in the butcher shop, where William supposedly killed calves "in a high style," making a speech for the occasion. It was this legendary William Shakespeare whose Falstaff (in *1* and *2 Henry IV*) so pleased Queen Elizabeth that she demanded a play about Falstaff in love, and demanded that it be written in fourteen days (hence the existence of *The Merry Wives of Windsor*). It was this legendary Shakespeare who reached the top of his acting career in the roles of the Ghost in *Hamlet* and old Adam in *As You Like It*—and who died of a fever contracted by drinking too hard at "a merry meeting" with the poets Michael Drayton and Ben Jonson. This legendary Shakespeare is a rambunctious, undisciplined man, as attractively "wild" as his plays were seen by earlier generations to be. Unfortunately, there is no trace of evidence to support these wonderful stories.

Perhaps in response to the disreputable Shakespeare of legend—or perhaps in response to the fragmentary and, for some, all-too-ordinary Shakespeare documented by surviving records—some people since the mid–nineteenth century have argued that William Shakespeare could not have written the plays that bear his name. These persons have put forward some dozen names as more likely authors, among them Queen Elizabeth, Sir Francis Bacon, Edward de Vere (earl of Oxford), and Christopher Marlowe. Such attempts to find what for these people is a more believable author of the plays is a tribute to the regard in which the plays are held. Unfortunately for their claims, the documents that exist that provide evidence for the facts of Shakespeare's life tie him inextricably to the body of plays and poems that bear his name. Unlikely as it seems to those who want the works to have been written by an aristocrat, a university graduate, or an "important" person, the plays and poems seem clearly to have been produced by a man from Stratford-upon-Avon with a very good "grammar school" education and a life of experience in London and in the world of the London theater. How this particular man produced the works that dominate the cultures of much of the world almost four hundred years after his death is one of life's mysteries—and one that will continue to tease our imaginations as we continue to delight in his plays and poems.

Shakespeare's Theater

The actors of Shakespeare's time performed plays in a great variety of locations. They played at court (that is, in the great halls of such royal residences as Whitehall, Hampton Court, and Greenwich); they played in halls at the universities of Oxford and Cambridge, and at the Inns of Court (the residences in London of the legal societies); and they also played in the private houses of great lords and civic officials. Sometimes acting companies went on tour from London into the provinces, often (but not only) when outbreaks of bubonic plague in the capital forced the closing of theaters to reduce the possibility of contagion in crowded audiences. In the provinces the actors usually staged their plays in churches (until around 1600) or in guildhalls. Though surviving records show only a handful of occasions when actors played at inns while on tour, London inns were important playing places up until the 1590s.

The building of theaters in London had begun only shortly before Shakespeare wrote his first plays in the 1590s. These theaters were of two kinds: outdoor or public playhouses that could accommodate large numbers of playgoers, and indoor or private theaters for much smaller audiences. What is usually regarded as the first London outdoor public playhouse was called simply the Theatre. James Burbage—the father of Richard Burbage, who was perhaps the most famous actor in Shakespeare's company—built it in 1576 in an area north of the city of London called Shoreditch. Among the more famous of the other public playhouses that capitalized on the new fashion were the Curtain and the Fortune (both also built north of the city), the Rose, the Swan, the Globe, and the Hope (all located on the Bankside, a region just across the Thames south of the city of London). All these playhouses had to be built outside the jurisdiction of the city of London because many civic officials were hostile to the performance of drama and repeatedly petitioned the royal council to abolish it.

The theaters erected on the Bankside (a region under the authority of the Church of England, whose head was the monarch) shared the neighborhood with houses of prostitution and with the Paris Garden, where the blood sports of bearbaiting and bullbaiting were carried on. There may have been no clear distinction between playhouses and buildings for such sports, for the Hope was used for both plays and baiting, and Philip Henslowe, owner of the Rose and, later, partner in the ownership of the Fortune, was also a partner in a monopoly on baiting. All these forms of entertainment were easily accessible to Londoners by boat across the Thames or over London Bridge.

Evidently Shakespeare's company prospered on the Bankside. They moved there in 1599. Threatened by difficulties in renewing the lease on the land where their first playhouse (the Theatre) had been built, Shakespeare's company took advantage of the Christmas holiday in 1598 to dismantle the Theatre and transport its timbers across the Thames to the Bankside, where, in 1599, these timbers were used in the building of the Globe. The weather in late December 1598 is recorded as having been especially harsh. It was so cold that the Thames was "nigh [nearly] frozen," and there was heavy snow. Perhaps the weather aided Shakespeare's company in eluding their landlord, the snow hiding their activity and the freezing of the Thames allowing them to slide the timbers across to the Bankside without paying tolls for repeated trips over London Bridge. Attractive as this narrative is, it remains just as likely that the heavy snow hampered transport of the timbers in wagons through the London streets to the river. It also must be remembered that the Thames was, according to report, only "nigh frozen" and therefore as impassable as it ever was. Whatever the precise circumstances of this fascinating event in English theater history, Shakespeare's company was able to begin playing at their new Globe theater on the Bankside in 1599. After the first Globe burned down in 1613 during the staging of Shakespeare's *Henry VIII* (its thatch roof was set alight by cannon fire called for by the performance), Shakespeare's company immediately rebuilt on the same location. The second Globe seems to have been a grander structure than its predecessor. It remained in use until the beginning of the English Civil War in 1642, when Parliament officially closed the theaters. Soon thereafter it was pulled down.

The public theaters of Shakespeare's time were very different buildings from our theaters today. First of all, they were open-air playhouses. As recent excavations of the Rose and the Globe confirm, some were polygonal or roughly circular in shape; the Fortune, however, was square. The most recent estimates of their size put the diameter of these buildings at 72 feet (the Rose) to 100 feet (the Globe), but they were said to hold vast audiences of two or three thousand, who must have been squeezed together quite tightly. Some of these spectators paid extra to sit or stand in the two or three levels of roofed galleries that extended, on the upper levels, all the way around the theater and surrounded an open space. In this space were the stage and, perhaps, the tiring house (what we would call dressing rooms), as well as the so-called yard. In the yard stood the spectators who chose to pay less, the ones whom Hamlet contemptuously called "groundlings." For a roof they had only the sky, and so they were exposed to all kinds of weather. They stood on a floor that was sometimes made of mortar and sometimes of ash mixed with the shells of hazelnuts. The latter provided a porous and therefore dry footing for the crowd, and the shells may have been more comfortable to stand on because they were not as hard as mortar. Availability of shells may not have been a problem if hazelnuts were a favorite food for Shakespeare's audiences to munch on as they watched his plays. Archaeologists who in the late 1980s unearthed the remains of theaters from this period discovered quantities of these nutshells on theater sites.

Unlike the yard, the stage itself was covered by a roof. Its ceiling, called "the heavens," is thought to have been elaborately painted to depict the sun, moon, stars, and planets. Just how big the stage was remains hard to determine. We have a single sketch of part of the interior of the Swan. A Dutchman named Johannes de Witt visited this theater around 1596 and sent a sketch of it back to his friend, Arend van Buchel. Because van Buchel found de Witt's letter and sketch of interest, he copied both into a book. It is van Buchel's copy, adapted, it seems, to the shape and size of the page in his book, that survives. In this sketch, the stage appears to be a large rectangular platform that thrusts far out into the yard, perhaps even as far as the center of the circle formed by the surrounding galleries. This drawing, combined with the specifications for the size of the stage in the building contract for the Fortune, has led scholars to conjecture that the stage on which Shakespeare's plays were performed must have measured approximately 43 feet in width and 27 feet in depth, a vast acting area. But the digging up of a large part of the Rose by archaeologists has provided evidence of a quite different stage design. The Rose stage was a platform tapered at the corners and much shallower than what seems to be depicted in the van Buchel sketch. Indeed, its measurements seem to be about 37.5 feet across at its widest point and only 15.5 feet deep. Because the surviving indications of stage size and design differ from each other so much, it is possible that the stages in other playhouses, like the Theatre, the Curtain, and the Globe (the outdoor playhouses where Shakespeare's plays were performed), were different from those at both the Swan and the Rose.

After about 1608 Shakespeare's plays were staged not only at the Globe but also at an indoor or private playhouse in Blackfriars. This theater had been constructed in 1596 by James Burbage in an upper hall of a former Dominican priory or monastic house. Although Henry VIII had dissolved all English monasteries in the 1530s (shortly after he had founded the Church of England), the area remained under church, rather than hostile civic, control. The hall that Burbage had purchased and renovated was a large one in which Parliament had once met. In the private theater that he constructed, the stage, lit by candles, was built across the narrow end of the hall, with boxes flanking it. The rest of the hall offered seating room only. Because there was no provision for standing room, the largest audience it could hold was less than a thousand, or about a quarter of what the Globe could accommodate. Admission to Blackfriars was correspondingly more expensive. Instead of a penny to stand in the yard at the Globe, it cost a minimum of sixpence to get into Blackfriars. The best seats at the Globe (in the Lords' Room in the gallery above and behind the stage) cost sixpence; but the boxes flanking the stage at Blackfriars were half a crown, or five times sixpence. Some spectators who were particularly interested in displaying themselves paid even more to sit on stools on the Blackfriars stage.

Whether in the outdoor or indoor playhouses, the stages of Shakespeare's time were different from ours. They were not separated from the audience by the dropping of a curtain between acts and scenes. Therefore the playwrights of the time had to find other ways of signaling to the audience that one scene (to be imagined as occurring in one location at a given time) had ended and the next (to be imagined at perhaps a different location at a later time) had begun. The customary way used by Shakespeare and many of his contemporaries was to have everyone onstage exit at the end of one scene and have one or more different characters enter to begin the next. In a few cases, where characters remain onstage from one scene to another, the dialogue or stage action makes the change of location clear, and the characters are generally to be imagined as having moved from one place to another. For example, in *Romeo and Juliet*, Romeo and his friends remain onstage in Act 1 from scene 4 to scene 5, but they are represented as having moved between scenes from the street that leads to Capulet's house into Capulet's house itself. The new location is signaled in part by the appearance onstage of Capulet's servingmen carrying napkins, something they would not take into the streets. Playwrights had to be quite resourceful in the use of hand properties, like the napkin, or in the use of dialogue to specify where the action was taking place in their plays because, in contrast to most of today's theaters, the playhouses of Shakespeare's time did not use movable scenery to dress the stage and make the setting precise. As another consequence of this difference, however, the playwrights of Shakespeare's time did not have to specify exactly where the action of their plays was set when they did not choose to do so, and much of the action of their plays is tied to no specific place.

Usually Shakespeare's stage is referred to as a "bare stage," to distinguish it from the stages of the past two or three centuries with their elaborate sets. But the stage in Shakespeare's time was not completely bare. Philip Henslowe, owner of the Rose, lists in his inventory of stage properties a rock, three tombs, and two mossy banks. Stage directions in plays of the time also call for such things as thrones (or "states"), banquets (presumably tables with plaster replicas of food on them), and beds and tombs to be pushed onto the stage. Thus the stage often held more than the actors.

The actors did not limit their performing to the stage alone. Occasionally they went beneath the stage, as the Ghost appears to do in the first act of *Hamlet*. From there they could emerge onto the stage through a trapdoor. They could retire behind the hangings across the back of the stage (or the front of the tiring house), as, for example, the actor playing Polonius does when he hides behind the arras. Sometimes the hangings could be drawn back during a performance to "discover" one or more actors behind them. When performance required that an actor appear "above," as when Juliet is imagined to stand at the window of her chamber in the famous and misnamed "balcony scene," then the actor probably climbed the stairs to the gallery over the back of the stage and temporarily shared it with some of the spectators. The stage was also provided with ropes and winches so that actors could descend from, and re-ascend to, the "heavens."

Perhaps the greatest difference between dramatic performances in Shakespeare's time and ours was that in Shakespeare's England the roles of women were played by boys. (Some of these boys grew up to take male roles in their maturity.) There were no women in the acting companies, only in the audience. It had not always been so in the history of the English stage. There are records of women on English stages in the thirteenth and fourteenth centuries, two hundred years before Shakespeare's plays were performed. After the accession of James I in 1603, the queen of England and her ladies took part in entertainments at court called masques, and with the reopening of the theaters in 1660 at the restoration of Charles II, women again took their place on the public stage.

The chief competitors for the companies of adult actors such as the one to which Shakespeare belonged and for which he wrote were companies of exclusively boy actors. The competition was most intense in the early 1600s. There were then two principal children's companies: the Children of Paul's (the choirboys from St. Paul's Cathedral, whose private playhouse was near the cathedral); and the Children of the Chapel Royal (the choirboys from the monarch's private chapel, who performed at the Blackfriars theater built by Burbage in 1596, which Shakespeare's company had been stopped from using by local residents who objected to crowds). In *Hamlet* Shakespeare writes of "an aerie [nest] of children, little eyases [hawks], that cry out on the top of question and are most tyrannically clapped for 't. These are now the fashion and . . . berattle the common stages [attack the public theaters]." In the long run, the adult actors prevailed. The Children of Paul's dissolved around 1606. By about 1608 the Children of the Chapel Royal had been forced to stop playing at the Blackfriars theater, which was then taken over by the King's company of players, Shakespeare's own troupe.

Acting companies and theaters of Shakespeare's time were organized in different ways. For example, Philip Henslowe owned the Rose and leased it to companies of actors, who paid him from their takings. Henslowe would act as manager of these companies, initially paying playwrights for their plays and buying properties, recovering his outlay from the actors. With the building of the Globe, however, Shakespeare's company managed itself, with the principal actors, Shakespeare among them, having the status of "sharers" and the right to a share in the takings, as well as the responsibility for a part of the expenses. Five of the sharers, including Shakespeare, owned the Globe. As actor, as sharer in an acting company and in ownership of theaters, and as playwright, Shakespeare was about as involved in the theatrical industry as one could imagine. Although Shakespeare and his fellows prospered, their status under the law was conditional upon the protection of powerful patrons. "Common players"— those who did not have patrons or masters—were classed in the language of the law with "vagabonds and sturdy beggars." So the actors had to secure for themselves the official rank of servants of patrons. Among the patrons under whose protection Shakespeare's company worked were the lord chamberlain and, after the accession of King James in 1603, the king himself.

In the early 1990s we seemed on the verge of learning a great deal more about the theaters in which Shakespeare and his contemporaries performed—or, at least, opening up new questions about them. At that time about 70 percent of the Rose had been excavated, as had about 10 percent of the second Globe, the one built in 1614. It was then hoped that more would become available for study. However, excavation was halted at that point, and it is not known if or when it will resume.

The Publication of Shakespeare's Plays

Eighteen of Shakespeare's plays found their way into print during the playwright's lifetime, but there is nothing to suggest that he took any interest in their publication. These eighteen appeared separately in editions called quartos. Their pages were not much larger than the one you are now reading, and these little books were sold unbound for a few pence. The earliest of the quartos that still survive were printed in 1594, the year that both *Titus Andronicus* and a version of the play now called *2 King Henry VI* became available. While almost every one of these early quartos displays on its title page the name of the acting company that performed the play, only about half provide the name of the playwright, Shakespeare. The first quarto edition to bear the name Shakespeare on its title page is *Love's Labor's Lost* of 1598. A few of these quartos were popular with the book-buying public of Shakespeare's lifetime; for example, quarto *Richard II* went through five editions between 1597 and 1615. But most of the quartos were far from best sellers; *Love's Labor's Lost* (1598), for instance, was not reprinted in quarto until 1631. After Shakespeare's death, two more of his plays appeared in quarto format: *Othello* in 1622 and *The Two Noble Kinsmen*, coauthored with John Fletcher, in 1634.

In 1623, seven years after Shakespeare's death, *Mr. William Shakespeares Comedies, Histories, & Tragedies* was published. This printing offered readers in a single book thirty-six of the thirty-eight plays now thought to have been written by Shakespeare, including eighteen that had never been printed before. And it offered them in a style that was then reserved for serious literature and scholarship. The plays were arranged in double columns on pages nearly a foot high. This large page size is called "folio," as opposed to the smaller "quarto," and the 1623 volume is usually called the Shakespeare First Folio. It is reputed to have sold for the lordly price of a pound. (One copy at the Folger Library is marked fifteen shillings—that is, three-quarters of a pound.)

In a preface to the First Folio entitled "To the great Variety of Readers," two of Shakespeare's former fellow actors in the King's Men, John Heminge and Henry Condell, wrote that they themselves had collected their dead companion's plays. They suggested that they had seen his own papers: "we have scarce received from him a blot in his papers." The title page of the Folio declared that the plays within it had been printed "according to the True Original Copies." Comparing the Folio to the quartos, Heminge and Condell disparaged the quartos, advising their readers that "before you were abused with divers stolen and surreptitious copies, maimed, and deformed by the frauds and stealths of injurious impostors." Many Shakespeareans

of the eighteenth and nineteenth centuries believed
Heminge and Condell and regarded the Folio plays as
superior to anything in the quartos.

Once we begin to examine the Folio plays in detail,
it becomes less easy to take at face value the word of
Heminge and Condell about the superiority of the
Folio texts. For example, of the first nine plays in the
Folio (one-quarter of the entire collection), four were
essentially reprinted from earlier quarto printings that
Heminge and Condell had disparaged; and four have
now been identified as printed from copies written in
the hand of a professional scribe of the 1620s named
Ralph Crane; the ninth, *The Comedy of Errors*, was
apparently also printed from a manuscript, but one
whose origin cannot be readily identified. Evidently,
then, eight of the first nine plays in the First Folio
were not printed, in spite of what the Folio title page
announces, "according to the True Original Copies," or
Shakespeare's own papers, and the source of the ninth
is unknown. Since today's editors have been forced to
treat Heminge and Condell's pronouncements with
skepticism, they must choose whether to base their
own editions upon quartos or the Folio on grounds
other than Heminge and Condell's story of where the
quarto and Folio versions originated.

Editors have often fashioned their own narratives
to explain what lies behind the quartos and Folio.
They have said that Heminge and Condell meant
to criticize only a few of the early quartos, the ones
that offer much shorter and sometimes quite different, often garbled, versions of plays. Among the
examples of these are the 1600 quarto of *Henry V* (the
Folio offers a much fuller version) or the 1603 *Hamlet* quarto (in 1604 a different, much longer form of
the play got into print as a quarto). Early-twentieth-
century editors speculated that these questionable

texts were produced when someone in the audience took notes from the plays' dialogue during performances and then employed "hack poets" to fill out the notes. The poor results were then sold to a publisher and presented in print as Shakespeare's plays. More recently this story has given way to another in which the shorter versions are said to be re-creations from memory of Shakespeare's plays by actors who wanted to stage them in the provinces but lacked manuscript copies. Most of the quartos offer much better texts than these so-called bad quartos. Indeed, in most of the quartos we find texts that are at least equal to or better than what is printed in the Folio. Many Shakespeare enthusiasts persuaded themselves that most of the quartos were set into type directly from Shakespeare's own papers, although there is nothing on which to base this conclusion except the desire for it to be true. Thus speculation continues about how the Shakespeare plays got to be printed. All that we have are the printed texts.

The book collector who was most successful in bringing together copies of the quartos and the First Folio was Henry Clay Folger, founder of the Folger Shakespeare Library in Washington, D.C. While it is estimated that there survive around the world only about 230 copies of the First Folio, Mr. Folger was able to acquire more than seventy-five copies, as well as a large number of fragments, for the library that bears his name. He also amassed a substantial number of quartos. For example, only fourteen copies of the First Quarto of *Love's Labor's Lost* are known to exist, and three are at the Folger Shakespeare Library. As a consequence of Mr. Folger's labors, scholars visiting the Folger Library have been able to learn a great deal about sixteenth- and seventeenth-century printing and, particularly, about the printing of Shakespeare's

THE LATE,

And much admired Play,

Called

Pericles, Prince
of Tyre.

With the true Relation of the whole Historie,
aduentures, and fortunes of the said Prince:
As also,
The no lesse strange, and worthy accidents,
in the Birth and Life, of his Daughter
MARIANA.

As it hath been diuers and sundry times acted by
his Maiesties Seruants, at the Globe on
the Banck-side.

By William ⬩⟨⟩⬩ Shakespeare.

George Steevens

Imprinted at London for *Henry Gosson,* and are
to be sold at the signe of the Sunne in
Pater-noster row, &c.
1 6 0 9.

Title page of the 1609 Quarto.
(From George Steevens's copy in the Folger Library Collection.)

plays. And Mr. Folger did not stop at the First Folio, but collected many copies of later editions of Shakespeare, beginning with the Second Folio (1632), the Third (1663–64), and the Fourth (1685). Each of these later folios was based on its immediate predecessor and was edited anonymously. The first editor of Shakespeare whose name we know was Nicholas Rowe, whose first edition came out in 1709. Mr. Folger collected this edition and many, many more by Rowe's successors.

An Introduction to This Text

Pericles was first published in a quarto of 1609 (Q) as *The late, and much admired Play, Called Pericles, Prince of Tyre*. The printing of Q was shared between two printing houses, one of which probably employed two different typesetters. A popular play, *Pericles* appeared in a second edition in the same year; Q2 was printed from Q and contained a few corrections and a few new errors. From Q2 was reprinted Q3 (1611), from Q3 was reprinted Q4 (1619), from Q4 came Q5 (1630), and from Q5 came Q6 (1635, but this time the printer also made use of a second earlier printing, Q4). When what we now call the Shakespeare First Folio was published in 1623, it contained no text of *Pericles*, which thus stands with *The Two Noble Kinsmen*, published in quarto in 1634, as one of only two plays not found in the First Folio that are widely accepted today as being of substantial Shakespearean authorship. *Pericles* was first printed in folio in the Third Folio (1663–64), as were several plays now thought to be wrongly attributed to Shakespeare. Its exclusion from the First Folio and inclusion in the Third among plays of doubtful authorship perhaps continues to color scholarly understanding of how Shakespearean *Pericles* may be.

Q's dialogue becomes unintelligible with a frequency that far exceeds that of other Shakespeare printed plays, besides those which scholars in the twentieth century called "bad quartos" (see page xlix). Its punctuation has also been called "chaotic" and its stage directions "vague." In addition, almost five hundred lines of its verse are printed as if they were prose; well over a hundred verse-lines are incorrectly divided. Some prose is also printed as verse. All these problems seem to worsen as one proceeds through Q. At the same time, there is a perceived heightening of Q's linguistic and dramatic excellence in the latter portion of the text.

A great many explanations for Q's condition have been put forward over the hundreds of years that Shakespeare's plays have been an object of study. Once *Pericles* was thought to be a very early work of Shakespeare's, written before his talent had matured. However, it was not printed until late in Shakespeare's career in 1609; there was no contemporary reference to its performance until sometime in the period 1606–08; and it bears many resemblances to Shakespeare's late plays *Cymbeline*, *The Winter's Tale*, and *The Tempest*. Thus scholars today place it late rather than early in Shakespeare's career, and no longer use a putative early production date to explain the text's condition. Other explanations trace the defects in Q's text to the multiplicity of agents supposed to be involved in its transmission into print. One suggestion is that the text was memorially reconstructed by two different reporters, one responsible for the first two acts (where the lining of verse and prose is relatively good), the other for the last three (where line division is a more severe problem). This suggestion has been countered by another that supposes the Q text to have been compiled from memory by two actors who took a variety of roles and had access to a written text of Gower's part (i.e., his lines). Both these suggestions must remain speculative, since we have no other text of the play to use for comparison with Q. Without such a text, it is impossible to judge if memory played a role in the transmission of the Q text or to tell which characters' speeches are transmitted more accurately. Only if the speeches of particular characters markedly exceed in accuracy those of others can we infer that particular actors memorially reconstructed a play. Shorthand, already developed in a number of forms by the early seventeenth century, has also been invoked as a method for the transmission of Q's text, but not persuasively.

Still other narratives of the origins of Q's peculiarly challenging text foreground multiple authorship. Advocates of this view account for differences between the first two acts and the last three—especially the perceived qualitative differences—by giving Shakespeare's collaborator the first two and Shakespeare all or most of the last three. Among the claimants for some or all of Acts 1–2 have been the dramatists William Rowley, Thomas Heywood, and John Day. Recently, the preferred candidate has been George Wilkins, the author of the 1608 prose work *The Painefull Aduentures of Pericles Prince of Tyre,* which advertises itself as "the true History of the Play of *Pericles*" "as it was vnder the habite of ancient *Gower* the famous English poet, by the Kings Maiesties Players excellently presented." Wilkins's novel is evidently, at least in part, a report of the play that was printed in 1609 in Q. (The weightiest presentation of the case for Wilkins as Shakespeare's collaborator in writing the play is MacDonald P. Jackson's *Defining Shakespeare: "Pericles" as Test Case* [Oxford: Oxford University Press, 2003].) However, in order to write the 1608 *The Painefull Aduentures,*

Wilkins borrowed extensively and often verbatim from Laurence Twine's *The Patterne of Painefull Aduentures* (1594, 1607), also a principal source for the play. (See the Appendix, page 207, for Twine's novel and John Gower's *Confessio Amantis* in the play.) If Wilkins had authored the play or any large part of it, it is odd that he would have had to engage in such borrowing. Not even Jackson can refute this objection. The origins of Q's text of the play remain, then, an intractable problem for Shakespeare scholars.

This present edition is based on the Q printing of the play.* For the convenience of the reader, we have modernized the punctuation and the spelling of Q. Sometimes we go so far as to modernize certain old forms of words; for example, usually when *a* means *he*, we change it to *he*; we change *mo* to *more*, and *ye* to *you*. But it is not our practice in editing any of the plays to modernize words that sound distinctly different from modern forms. For example, when the early printed texts read *sith* or *apricocks* or *porpentine*, we have not modernized to *since*, *apricots*, *porcupine*. When the forms *an*, *and*, or *and if* appear instead of the modern form *if*, we have reduced *and* to *an* but have not changed any of these forms to their modern equivalent, *if*. We also modernize and, where necessary, correct passages in foreign languages, unless an error in the early printed text can be reasonably explained as a joke.

Whenever we change the wording of Q or add anything to Q's stage directions, we mark the change by enclosing it in superior half-brackets (⌈ ⌉). We employ these brackets because we want our readers to be immediately aware when we have intervened. (Only

---

*We have also consulted the computerized text of Q on the website of Michael Best, ed., *Internet Shakespeare Editions*, University of Victoria, Canada.

when we correct an obvious typographical error in Q does the change not get marked.) Whenever we change either the wording of Q or its punctuation so that meaning changes, we list the change in the textual notes at the back of the book, even if all we have done is fix an obvious error.

We regularize spellings of a number of the proper names, as is the usual practice in editions of the play. For example, Q calls the King of Pentapolis sometimes "Simonides," sometimes "Simonydes," and sometimes "Symonides," but we use the spelling "Simonides" throughout the text. We also expand the often severely abbreviated forms of names used as speech headings in early printed texts into the full names of the characters. Changes to the speech headings of the early printed texts are recorded in the textual notes.

This edition differs from many earlier ones in its efforts to aid the reader in imagining the play as a performance rather than as a series of actual events. For example, in 1 Chorus, Gower verbally gestures to the severed heads of the suitors who have failed in the contest to marry Antiochus's daughter and forfeited their lives: "for her many a wight did die, / As yon grim looks do testify" (lines 39–40). In the fiction of the play, these heads have been placed on the palace walls, and many editors write a stage direction to accompany Gower's words that refers to the fictional location of these heads "on the walls." But because we wish to encourage readers to imagine the play as performance, rather than simply as fiction, we word this stage direction somewhat differently: *"He indicates heads above the stage."*

Whenever, as here, it is reasonably certain, in our view, that a speech is accompanied by a particular action, we provide a stage direction describing the action, setting the added direction in brackets to signal that it is not found in Q. (Exceptions to this rule occur when the action is so obvious that to add a stage direction would insult the reader.) Stage directions for the entrance of a character in mid-scene are, with rare exceptions, placed so that they immediately precede the character's participation in the scene, even though these entrances may appear somewhat earlier in the early printed texts. Whenever we move a stage direction, we record this change in the textual notes. Latin stage directions (e.g., *Exeunt*) are translated into English (e.g., *They exit*).

In the present edition, as well, we mark with a dash any change of address within a speech, unless a stage direction intervenes. When the -ed ending of a word is to be pronounced, we mark it with an accent. Like editors for the past two centuries, we print each metrically linked line (provided the linked lines produce a pentameter) in the following way:

SECOND GENTLEMAN
    Most likely, sir.
CERIMON   Nay, certainly tonight[.]
                                              (3.2.89–90)

However, when there are a number of short verse-lines that can be linked in more than one way to produce a pentameter line, we do not, with rare exceptions, indent any of them.

The Explanatory Notes

The notes that appear on the pages facing the text are designed to provide readers with the help that they may need to enjoy the play. Whenever the meaning of a word in the text is not readily accessible in a good contemporary dictionary, we offer the meaning in a note. Sometimes we provide a note even when the relevant meaning is to be found in the dictionary but when the word has acquired since Shakespeare's time other potentially confusing meanings. In our notes, we try to offer modern synonyms for Shakespeare's words. We also try to indicate to the reader the connection between the word in the play and the modern synonym. For example, Shakespeare sometimes uses the word *head* to mean *source*, but, for modern readers, there may be no connection evident between these two words. We provide the connection by explaining Shakespeare's usage as follows: "**head:** fountainhead, source." On some occasions, a whole phrase or clause needs explanation. Then, when space allows, we rephrase in our own words the difficult passage, and add at the end synonyms for individual words in the passage. When scholars have been unable to determine the meaning of a word or phrase, we acknowledge the uncertainty. Whenever we provide a passage from the Bible to illuminate the text of the play, we use the Geneva Bible of 1560 (with spelling modernized).

PERICLES,

Prince of Tyre

Characters in the Play

GOWER, fourteenth-century poet and Chorus of the play

PERICLES, prince of Tyre
THAISA, princess of Pentapolis and wife to Pericles
MARINA, daughter of Pericles and Thaisa

HELICANUS ⎫
ESCANES ⎭ lords of Tyre
Three other LORDS of Tyre

ANTIOCHUS, king of Antioch
DAUGHTER, princess of Antioch
THALIARD, nobleman of Antioch
MESSENGER

CLEON, governor of Tarsus
DIONYZA, wife to Cleon
LEONINE, servant to Dionyza
A LORD of Tarsus
Three PIRATES

SIMONIDES, king of Pentapolis
Three FISHERMEN
MARSHAL
Five KNIGHTS, suitors for the hand of Thaisa
LORDS of Pentapolis
LYCHORIDA, attendant to Thaisa and, later, to Marina
Two SAILORS, mariners onboard ship from Pentapolis

LORD CERIMON, a wiseman/physician in Ephesus
PHILEMON, servant to Cerimon
Two SUPPLIANTS
Two GENTLEMEN of Ephesus
SERVANT

3

DIANA, goddess of chastity

LYSIMACHUS, governor of Mitylene
PANDER, owner of brothel
BAWD, mistress of brothel and wife to Pander
BOLT, servant to Pander and Bawd
Two GENTLEMEN, visitors to brothel

Tyrian SAILOR
SAILOR from Mytilene
GENTLEMAN of Tyre
LORD of Mytilene

Followers of Antiochus, Attendants to Pericles, Attendants to Simonides, Squires to the five Knights, Tyrian gentlemen, Citizens of Tarsus, Ladies of Pentapolis, Servants to Cerimon, Companion to Marina, Priestesses in Diana's temple, Messenger from Tyre

PERICLES,

Prince of Tyre

ACT 1

1 Chorus Gower sets the stage for Pericles' entrance at Antioch by telling of the incest between Antiochus and his daughter, whom Pericles seeks to marry.

---

1. **sing a song:** i.e., recite a poem, tell a story; **old:** long ago, in ancient times

2. **ashes:** i.e., the tomb; **Gower:** John **Gower** was a 14th-century poet who, in his *Confessio Amantis,* wrote one of the versions of the story told in *Pericles.* (See picture, page 188, and Appendix, page 207.)

4. **glad:** i.e., make glad (**Gower** is given archaic language and speaks in a verse form modeled on the *Confessio.*)

6. **ember eves:** vigils of **Ember** days (special periods of fasting and prayer)

9. **purchase:** gain, benefit; **glorious:** eager for glory

10. **Et . . . melius:** Proverbial: "And the older a good thing is, the better" (Latin).

12. **wit's more ripe:** i.e., wisdom or understanding is more mature

16. **Waste:** spend, expend

17. **Antioch:** See map, page xii.

18. **seat:** city where his throne was set; capital

20. **mine authors:** i.e., the authorities from whose books I draw this story

21. **a peer:** i.e., a wife (literally, an equal in rank)

6

⌜ACT 1⌝

Enter Gower.

⌜GOWER⌝
To sing a song that old was sung,
From ashes ancient Gower is come,
Assuming man's infirmities
To glad your ear and please your eyes.
It hath been sung at festivals,   5
On ember eves and holy days,
And lords and ladies in their lives
Have read it for restoratives.
The purchase is to make men glorious,
Et bonum quo antiquius, eo melius.   10
If you, born in ⌜these⌝ latter times
When wit's more ripe, accept my rhymes,
And that to hear an old man sing
May to your wishes pleasure bring,
I life would wish, and that I might   15
Waste it for you like taper light.
This Antioch, then: Antiochus the Great
Built up this city for his chiefest seat,
The fairest in all Syria.
I tell you what mine authors say.   20
This king unto him took a peer,
Who died and left a female heir

7

23. **buxom:** bright, lively; **full:** perfect

24. **As:** i.e., as if; **his:** its

28. **should:** i.e., that **should**

29–30. **custom . . . sin:** Proverbial: **"Custom** of **sin** makes no **sin."**

32. **frame:** i.e., journey

36. **still:** always

38. **His riddle told not:** i.e., if he could not discern the meaning of the king's **riddle**

39. **wight:** creature

42. **I give my cause:** perhaps, I submit my case or suit; **who:** i.e., you **who; justify:** judge

1.1 Pericles risks his life to win the hand of Antiochus's daughter, but, in meeting the challenge, he learns of the incest between her and her father. In mortal danger, he flees Antioch. Antiochus sends Thaliard to kill Pericles.

————————

1. **at large received:** heard in full

So buxom, blithe, and full of face
As heaven had lent her all his grace;
With whom the father liking took   25
And her to incest did provoke.
Bad child, worse father! To entice his own
To evil should be done by none.
But custom what they did begin
Was with long use accounted no sin.   30
The beauty of this sinful dame
Made many princes thither frame
To seek her as a bedfellow,
In marriage pleasures playfellow;
Which to prevent he made a law   35
To keep her still, and men in awe,
That whoso asked her for his wife,
His riddle told not, lost his life.
So for her many ⌜a⌝ wight did die,
As yon grim looks do testify.   40
                 ⌜*He indicates heads above the stage.*⌝
What now ensues, to the judgment of your eye
I give my cause, who best can justify.
                                        He exits.

                        ⌜Scene 1⌝

    Enter Antiochus, Prince Pericles, and followers.

ANTIOCHUS
  Young Prince of Tyre, you have at large received
  The danger of the task you undertake.
PERICLES
  I have, Antiochus, and with a soul
  Emboldened with the glory of her praise
  Think death no hazard in this enterprise.   5

7. **our:** i.e., my (Antiochus uses the royal plural throughout when speaking to others.)

8. **Jove:** king of the Roman gods (See picture, page 24.)

9. **At . . . reigned:** i.e., from the daughter's **conception** to her birth **Lucina:** the Roman goddess of childbirth (See picture, page 96.)

10. **to glad her presence:** perhaps, to make her happy; or, perhaps, to make her delightful to others

11–12. **senate . . . perfections:** In this image, the stars and **planets,** which were thought to control human destiny, meet as a governing body to bestow on the daughter their most favorable aspects.

14. **Graces:** the mythological sister-goddesses who bestowed beauty and charm, here the **subjects** of the daughter (See picture, page 66.)

15. **gives:** i.e., that **gives**

17. **curious:** exquisite; **as:** as though

18. **ever razed:** forever erased or obliterated; **testy:** contentious

22. **taste the fruit:** See note to **Hesperides,** line 28.

25. **compass:** (1) seize; (2) embrace

28. **Hesperides:** for Shakespeare and other poets, the name of a mythological garden in which **golden** apples grew (Literally, the **Hesperides** were the nymphs who, with a dragon, guarded the apples.) See picture, page 70.

30. **deathlike:** deadly; **affright:** frighten, terrify

32. **countless:** i.e., incalculable; **desert:** worthiness, excellence

33. **without desert:** i.e., if you are not worthy

ANTIOCHUS
  Music! ⌜*Music sounds offstage.*⌝
  Bring in our daughter, clothèd like a bride
  For embracements even of Jove himself,
  At whose conception, till Lucina reigned,
  Nature this dowry gave: to glad her presence,   10
  The senate house of planets all did sit
  To knit in her their best perfections.

             Enter Antiochus' daughter.

PERICLES
  See where she comes, appareled like the spring,
  Graces her subjects, and her thoughts the king
  Of every virtue gives renown to men!   15
  Her face the book of praises, where is read
  Nothing but curious pleasures, as from thence
  Sorrow were ever ⌜razed⌝, and testy wrath
  Could never be her mild companion.
  You gods that made me man, and sway in love,   20
  That have inflamed desire in my breast
  To taste the fruit of yon celestial tree
  Or die in th' adventure, be my helps,
  As I am son and servant to your will,
  To compass such a boundless happiness.   25

ANTIOCHUS
  Prince Pericles—

PERICLES
  That would be son to great Antiochus.

ANTIOCHUS
  Before thee stands this fair Hesperides,
  With golden fruit, but dangerous to be touched;
  For deathlike dragons here affright thee hard.   30
  Her face, like heaven, enticeth thee to view
  Her countless glory, which desert must gain;
  And which without desert, because thine eye
  Presumes to reach, all the whole heap must die.

35. **Yon:** i.e., those; **sometimes:** i.e., sometime, formerly

36. **advent'rous by:** rashly daring because of

37. **semblance:** appearance

39. **Cupid's:** i.e., love's (In Roman mythology, Cupid was the god of love.)

41. **For going on:** perhaps, from entering

45. **like to:** i.e., **like; must:** i.e., **must** someday be

47. **Who:** i.e., which (See picture, page 72.)

50. **Gripe:** clutch, grasp; **erst:** not long ago

54. **unspotted:** pure

58. **conclusion:** riddle, enigma

61. **'sayed yet:** i.e., who have **yet** assayed or endeavored; or, who have so far been tested; **prosperous:** successful

63. **assume the lists:** i.e., prepare to do battle (Tournaments and tilting matches were held in an enclosure called **the lists.**) See picture below.

Combat in the lists. (1.1.63)
From [Sir William Segar,] *The booke of honor and armes* . . . (1590).

⌜*He points to the heads.*⌝

Yon sometimes famous princes, like thyself,   35
Drawn by report, advent'rous by desire,
Tell thee with speechless tongues and semblance pale
That, without covering save yon field of stars,
Here they stand martyrs slain in Cupid's wars,
And with dead cheeks advise thee to desist   40
For going on death's net, whom none resist.

PERICLES
Antiochus, I thank thee, who hath taught
My frail mortality to know itself,
And by those fearful objects to prepare
This body, like to them, to what I must.   45
For death remembered should be like a mirror
Who tells us life's but breath, to trust it error.
I'll make my will, then, and as sick men do
Who know the world, see heaven but, feeling woe,
Gripe not at earthly joys as erst they did;   50
So I bequeath a happy peace to you
And all good men, as every prince should do;
My riches to the earth from whence they came,
⌜*To the Daughter.*⌝ But my unspotted fire of love to
    you.—   55
Thus ready for the way of life or death,
I wait the sharpest blow.

ANTIOCHUS
Scorning advice, read the conclusion, then:
Which read and not expounded, 'tis decreed,
As these before thee, thou thyself shalt bleed.   60

DAUGHTER
Of all 'sayed yet, mayst thou prove prosperous;
Of all 'sayed yet, I wish thee happiness.

PERICLES
Like a bold champion I assume the lists,
Nor ask advice of any other thought
But faithfulness and courage.   65

66–67. **I . . . breed:** an allusion to the belief that vipers were born by eating their way out through the **mother's flesh**

72. **they:** i.e., the six roles of **father, son,** etc.; **in two:** i.e., **in** (only) **two** (persons)

74. **Sharp physic:** harsh medicine

75. **gives:** i.e., give

78. **glass of light:** i.e., lantern, **glass** vessel that gives **light** (This image of the daughter as a glowing lantern is replaced in line 79 with that of a **casket**—a jewelry box—filled with evil.)

81. **perfections wait:** i.e., virtues attend

83. **sense:** senses

84. **Who:** i.e., which

86. **hearken:** listen, pay attention

88. **Hell only:** i.e., **only Hell; chime:** musical sound

89. **Good sooth:** i.e., truly, indeed

90. **touch not:** Pericles apparently makes a gesture that Antiochus misinterprets.

96. **braid yourself:** upbraid or reproach you; **near:** closely, directly; **tell:** reveal, disclose

97. **Who:** i.e., he **who,** whoever

99. **repeated:** related, recounted

100. **Blows:** i.e., which **blows** (The image is an ambiguous one because "to blow **dust** in someone's **eyes**" has a secondary meaning, "to deceive someone.")

⌈*He reads*⌉ *the Riddle:*
> *I am no viper, yet I feed*
> *On mother's flesh which did me breed.*
> *I sought a husband, in which labor*
> *I found that kindness in a father.*
> *He's father, son, and husband mild;* 70
> *I mother, wife, and yet his child.*
> *How they may be, and yet in two,*
> *As you will live resolve it you.*

⌈*Aside.*⌉ Sharp physic is the last! But, O you powers
That gives heaven countless eyes to view men's acts, 75
Why cloud they not their sights perpetually
If this be true which makes me pale to read it?
Fair glass of light, I loved you, and could still
Were not this glorious casket stored with ill.
But I must tell you now my thoughts revolt; 80
For he's no man on whom perfections wait
That, knowing sin within, will touch the gate.
You are a fair viol, and your sense the strings
Who, fingered to make man his lawful music,
Would draw heaven down and all the gods to 85
    hearken;
But, being played upon before your time,
Hell only danceth at so harsh a chime.
Good sooth, I care not for you.

ANTIOCHUS
Prince Pericles, touch not, upon thy life, 90
For that's an article within our law
As dangerous as the rest. Your time's expired.
Either expound now or receive your sentence.

PERICLES   Great king,
Few love to hear the sins they love to act. 95
'Twould braid yourself too near for me to tell it.
Who has a book of all that monarchs do,
He's more secure to keep it shut than shown.
For vice repeated is like the wand'ring wind,
Blows dust in others' eyes to spread itself; 100

101. **thus dear: thus** dearly, at this expense

102. **The breath:** i.e., the gossiper's **breath; see clear:** i.e., **see** clearly how

103. **the air would hurt them:** i.e., the **dust**-filled wind that **would hurt** the eyes

104. **Copped:** peaked; **tell:** i.e., recount that

106. **worm:** creature (either the **mole** itself or the earthworm that is its food) See picture below.

109. **ill:** evil

110. **you:** i.e., that **you**

113. **like leave:** similar permission

116. **gloze:** i.e., use smooth or flattering words

118. **misinterpreting:** i.e., being a misinterpretation

119. **cancel of:** i.e., **cancel**

120. **succeeding:** proceeding

125. **entertain:** treatment as a guest

127. **seem to:** i.e., dissemble in order to

129. **sight:** appearance

133. **Where:** i.e., whereas

A mole. (1.1.103)
From Edward Topsell, *The historie of foure-footed beastes . . .* (1607).

And yet the end of all is bought thus dear:
The breath is gone, and the sore eyes see clear
To stop the air would hurt them. The blind mole casts
Copped hills towards heaven, to tell the earth is
   thronged   105
By man's oppression, and the poor worm doth die
   for 't.
Kings are earth's gods; in vice their law's their will;
And if Jove stray, who dares say Jove doth ill?
It is enough you know; and it is fit,   110
What being more known grows worse, to smother it.
All love the womb that their first being bred;
Then give my tongue like leave to love my head.

ANTIOCHUS, ⌐*aside*¬

Heaven, that I had thy head! He has found the
   meaning.   115
But I will gloze with him.—Young Prince of Tyre,
Though by the tenor of ⌐our¬ strict edict,
Your exposition misinterpreting,
We might proceed to ⌐cancel¬ of your days,
Yet hope, succeeding from so fair a tree   120
As your fair self, doth tune us otherwise.
Forty days longer we do respite you,
If by which time our secret be undone,
This mercy shows we'll joy in such a son.
And until then, your entertain shall be   125
As doth befit our honor and your worth.
                         All except Pericles exit.

PERICLES

How courtesy would seem to cover sin
When what is done is like an hypocrite,
The which is good in nothing but in sight.
If it be true that I interpret false,   130
Then were it certain you were not so bad
As with foul incest to abuse your soul;
Where now ⌐you're¬ both a father and a son

134. **untimely claspings:** As line 87 notes, the daughter has been "played upon before [her] time."

135. **fits:** i.e., fit

140. **those men:** i.e., that **those men** who

142. **'schew:** i.e., eschew, avoid; **them:** i.e., the **actions**

146. **targets to put off:** perhaps, shields to deflect (See picture, page 74.)

158. **of our chamber:** i.e., my chamberlain, one who attends me in my private **chamber** (**Thaliard** would thus be a man of high rank who is of the king's inner circle.)

159. **partakes:** imparts, communicates

A serpent in a strawberry plant. (1.1.138–39)
From Claude Paradin, *The heroicall deuises* . . . (1591).

By your untimely claspings with your child,
Which pleasures fits a husband, not a father,   135
And she an eater of her mother's flesh
By the defiling of her parents' bed;
And both like serpents are, who, though they feed
On sweetest flowers, yet they poison breed.
Antioch, farewell, for wisdom sees those men   140
Blush not in actions blacker than the night
Will ⌜'schew⌝ no course to keep them from the light.
One sin, I know, another doth provoke;
Murder's as near to lust as flame to smoke.
Poison and treason are the hands of sin,   145
Ay, and the targets to put off the shame.
Then, lest my life be cropped to keep you clear,
By flight I'll shun the danger which I fear.   *He exits.*

Enter Antiochus.

ANTIOCHUS   He hath found the meaning,
For which we mean to have his head.   150
He must not live to trumpet forth my infamy,
Nor tell the world Antiochus doth sin
In such a loathèd manner.
And therefore instantly this prince must die,
For by his fall my honor must keep high.—   155
Who attends us there?

Enter Thaliard.

THALIARD   Doth your Highness call?
ANTIOCHUS
Thaliard, you are of our chamber, Thaliard,
And our mind partakes her private actions
To your secrecy; and for your faithfulness   160
We will advance you, Thaliard. Behold,
Here's poison, and here's gold. ⌜*He gives poison and
money.*⌝ We hate the Prince
Of Tyre, and thou must kill him. It fits thee not

169. **telling your haste:** i.e., as you explain the reason for **your haste** (The line could be addressed to the Messenger or to Thaliard.)

173. **level:** aim (See picture below.)

177. **length:** range; **make . . . enough:** put him well beyond the power of doing harm; do away with him

180. **succor:** help

1.2 Back in his kingdom of Tyre, Pericles, fearing the power of Antiochus, sets sail once again.

---

1. **us:** i.e., me (the royal plural)

4. **used:** accustomed, usual

5. **day's . . . walk:** i.e., sun's . . . journey (through the sky)

6. **breed me:** i.e., produce for me, create in me, cause me to become

An archer aiming at the mark. (1.1.172–73; 2.3.121)
From Gilles Corrozet, *Hecatongraphie* . . . (1543).

To ask the reason why: because we bid it.   165
Say, is it done?
THALIARD   My lord, 'tis done.
ANTIOCHUS   Enough.

Enter a Messenger.

Let your breath cool yourself, telling your haste.
MESSENGER   My lord, Prince Pericles is fled. ⌜*He exits.*⌝ 170
ANTIOCHUS, ⌜*to Thaliard*⌝ As thou wilt live, fly after,
     and like an arrow shot from a well-experienced
     archer hits the mark his eye doth level at, so thou
     never return unless thou say Prince Pericles is
     dead.   175
THALIARD   My lord, if I can get him within my pistol's
     length, I'll make him sure enough. So, farewell to
     your Highness.
⌜ANTIOCHUS⌝
Thaliard, adieu. Till Pericles be dead,
My heart can lend no succor to my head.   180
                                        ⌜*They exit.*⌝

⌜Scene 2⌝

Enter Pericles with ⌜an Attendant.⌝

PERICLES
Let none disturb us. (⌜*Attendant exits.*⌝) Why should
     this change of thoughts,
The sad companion dull-eyed Melancholy,
⌜Be my⌝ so used a guest as not an hour
In the day's glorious walk or peaceful night,   5
The tomb where grief should sleep, can breed me
     quiet?
Here pleasures court mine eyes, and mine eyes shun
     them;
And danger, which I feared, is at Antioch,   10

11. **arm . . . short:** Proverbial: "Kings have long arms."

12. **art:** skill (in courting or seducing, line 8)

14. **passions:** i.e., overpowering emotions

15. **misdread:** perhaps, dread of evil (This is the only recorded usage of this word.)

16. **by care:** i.e., through anxiety

17. **what:** i.e., that something

21. **can make:** i.e., that he **can make**

23. **boots it me:** i.e., does it help me

25. **known:** i.e., generally **known,** made public

28. **ostent:** display

29. **Amazement:** terror, overwhelming fear

34. **fence:** shield, screen, protect; **they grow by:** i.e., **by** which the trees are able to **grow**

38. **till you return to us:** This is a puzzling statement, since, in the following scene, the lords know nothing of Pericles' plan to leave. (Some modern editions cut the statement.) See longer note, page 191.

40. **give experience tongue:** perhaps, let **experience** speak

Whose arm seems far too short to hit me here.
Yet neither pleasure's art can joy my spirits,
Nor yet the other's distance comfort me.
Then it is thus: the passions of the mind
That have their first conception by misdread   15
Have after-nourishment and life by care;
And what was first but fear what might be done
Grows elder now, and cares it be not done.
And so with me. The great Antiochus,
'Gainst whom I am too little to contend,   20
Since he's so great can make his will his act,
Will think me speaking though I swear to silence;
Nor boots it me to say I honor ⌜him⌝
If he suspect I may dishonor him.
And what may make him blush in being known,   25
He'll stop the course by which it might be known.
With hostile forces he'll o'er-spread the land,
And with ⌜th' ostent⌝ of war will look so huge
Amazement shall drive courage from the state,
Our men be vanquished ere they do resist,   30
And subjects punished that ne'er thought offense;
Which care of them, not pity of myself,
Who ⌜am⌝ no more but as the tops of trees
Which fence the roots they grow by and defend them,
Makes both my body pine and soul to languish   35
And punish that before that he would punish.

Enter ⌜Helicanus and⌝ all the Lords to Pericles.

FIRST LORD
    Joy and all comfort in your sacred breast.
SECOND LORD
    And keep your mind till you return to us
    Peaceful and comfortable.
HELICANUS
    Peace, peace, and give experience tongue.   40
    They do abuse the King that flatter him,

42. **blows up:** i.e., which inflames

43. **the which:** i.e., **which; but:** is only

46. **Fits:** is appropriate or suitable for

47. **Signior Sooth:** Sir Flattery (See longer note to 1.2.38, page 191.)

51. **cares:** attention, concern; **o'erlook:** inspect, examine

55. **moved us:** i.e., made me angry

58. **durst . . . face:** i.e., did your **tongue** dare openly to incite my **anger**

Jove. (1.1.8, 109; 2.3.31; 3.1.4–6)
From Vincenzo Cartari, *Le vere e noue imagini* . . . (1615).

For flattery is the bellows blows up sin;
The thing the which is flattered, but a spark
To which that ⌜wind⌝ gives heat and stronger glowing;
Whereas reproof, obedient and in order, 45
Fits kings as they are men, for they may err.
When Signior Sooth here does proclaim peace,
He flatters you, makes war upon your life.
⌜*He kneels.*⌝

Prince, pardon me, or strike me, if you please.
I cannot be much lower than my knees. 50

PERICLES
All leave us else; but let your cares o'erlook
What shipping and what lading's in our haven,
And then return to us. ⌜*The Lords exit.*⌝
    Helicanus,
Thou hast moved us. What seest thou in our looks? 55

HELICANUS An angry brow, dread lord.

PERICLES
If there be such a dart in princes' frowns,
How durst thy tongue move anger to our face?

HELICANUS
How dares the plants look up to heaven,
From whence they have their nourishment? 60

PERICLES
Thou knowest I have power to take thy life from thee.

HELICANUS I have ground the ax myself;
Do but you strike the blow.

PERICLES
Rise, prithee rise. ⌜*Helicanus rises.*⌝
    Sit down. Thou art no flatterer. 65
I thank thee for 't; and heaven forbid
That kings should let their ears hear their faults hid.
Fit counselor and servant for a prince,
Who by thy wisdom makes a prince thy servant,
What wouldst thou have me do? 70

HELICANUS To bear with patience such griefs
As you yourself do lay upon yourself.

76. **Attend:** listen to
78. **purchase:** acquisition
79. **an issue:** i.e., offspring (here, royal descendants)
80. **Are:** i.e., who or which **are**
84. **smooth:** i.e., put on a conciliatory manner
88. **careful:** watchful, solicitous
89. **Who:** i.e., which
90. **Bethought me:** called to my mind
93. **he doubt:** i.e., he fear
94. **open:** reveal, make known
96. **unlaid ope:** i.e., hidden, secret (literally, not laid open)
97. **lop that doubt:** i.e., cut off that fear
99. **all:** i.e., **all** of my subjects
100. **who:** i.e., which
102. **now:** i.e., just **now**
107. **them:** i.e., the **doubts** (line 105)

"Dull-eyed Melancholy." (1.2.3)
From Cesare Ripa, *Iconologia* . . . (1611).

PERICLES
  Thou speak'st like a physician, Helicanus,
  That ministers a potion unto me
  That thou wouldst tremble to receive thyself.   75
  Attend me, then: I went to Antioch,
  Where, as thou know'st, against the face of death
  I sought the purchase of a glorious beauty
  From whence an issue I might propagate,
  Are arms to princes and bring joys to subjects.   80
  Her face was to mine eye beyond all wonder,
  The rest—hark in thine ear—as black as incest,
  Which by my knowledge found, the sinful father
  Seemed not to strike, but smooth. But thou know'st
    this: 85
  'Tis time to fear when tyrants seems to kiss;
  Which fear so grew in me I hither fled
  Under the covering of a careful night,
  Who seemed my good protector; and, being here,
  Bethought ⌜me⌝ what was past, what might succeed.   90
  I knew him tyrannous, and tyrants' ⌜fears⌝
  Decrease not but grow faster than the years;
  And should he ⌜doubt,⌝ as no doubt he doth,
  That I should open to the list'ning air
  How many worthy princes' bloods were shed   95
  To keep his bed of blackness unlaid ope,
  To lop that doubt he'll fill this land with arms,
  And make pretense of wrong that I have done him;
  When all, for mine—if I may ⌜call 't⌝—offense,
  Must feel war's blow, who spares not innocence;   100
  Which love to all—of which thyself art one,
  Who now reproved'st me for 't—
HELICANUS Alas, sir!
PERICLES
  Drew sleep out of mine eyes, blood from my cheeks,
  Musings into my mind, with thousand doubts   105
  How I might stop this tempest ere it came;
  And finding little comfort to relieve them,

108. **them:** i.e., **all** his subjects (line 101)

116. **Destinies:** a name given the three mythological goddesses (also called **Fates** [3.3.9, 4.3.14]) who determine the course of a person's life (See picture, page 182.)

117. **direct:** delegate

119. **faith:** allegiance, fealty; loyalty

120. **liberties:** perhaps, (royal) prerogatives; perhaps, territories; perhaps, (subjects') freedoms

123. **Tyre, Tarsus:** See map, page xii.

124. **Intend:** direct

129. **Who shuns not to break:** i.e., he **who** does not guard against breaking

130–32. **But . . . prince:** These lines are very obscure, in part because a line is apparently missing before or after line 130 (to rhyme with "safe"). **orbs:** spheres of action (In Ptolemaic cosmology, each planet was thought to circle around the earth in its orb or sphere. See picture, page 176.) **round:** i.e., honestly, straightforwardly (with wordplay on the circular motion of the orb) **convince:** confute **shine:** luster, splendor

1.3 Thaliard arrives in Tyre to find Pericles gone.

    I thought it princely charity to grieve for them.

HELICANUS
    Well, my lord, since you have given me leave to speak,
    Freely will I speak. Antiochus you fear,   110
    And justly too, I think, you fear the tyrant,
    Who either by public war or private treason
    Will take away your life.
    Therefore, my lord, go travel for a while,
    Till that his rage and anger be forgot,   115
    Or till the Destinies do cut his thread of life.
    Your rule direct to any. If to me,
    Day serves not light more faithful than I'll be.

PERICLES   I do not doubt thy faith.
    But should he wrong my liberties in my absence?   120

HELICANUS
    We'll mingle our bloods together in the earth,
    From whence we had our being and our birth.

PERICLES
    Tyre, I now look from thee, then, and to Tarsus
    Intend my travel, where I'll hear from thee,
    And by whose letters I'll dispose myself.   125
    The care I had and have of subjects' good
    On thee I lay, whose wisdom's strength can bear it.
    I'll take thy word for faith, not ask thine oath.
    Who shuns not to break one will crack both.
    But in our orbs ⌜we'll⌝ live so round and safe   130
    That time of both this truth shall ne'er convince.
    Thou showed'st a subject's shine, I a true prince.
                              ⌜*They*⌝ *exit.*

⌜Scene 3⌝

Enter Thaliard alone.

⌜THALIARD⌝ So this is Tyre, and this the court. Here
    must I kill King Pericles; and if I do it not, I am

4–6. **he was . . . secrets:** The man referred to is the ancient poet Philippides. **discretion:** judgment **bid:** commanded **would of:** i.e., wanted from

9. **indenture:** contract (literally, a contract between master and servant)

13. **sealed commission:** i.e., **commission** bearing the royal seal

17. **unlicensed of your loves:** i.e., without license (permission) from you, his loving subjects

23. **doubting lest:** fearing that

28. **although I would:** i.e., even if I wanted to be

sure to be hanged at home. 'Tis dangerous. Well, I
perceive he was a wise fellow and had good discretion that, being bid to ask what he would of the   5
king, desired he might know none of his secrets.
Now do I see he had some reason for 't, for if a
king bid a man be a villain, he's bound by the
indenture of his oath to be one. Husht! Here
comes the lords of Tyre.   ⌜*He steps aside.*⌝   10

Enter Helicanus ⌜and⌝ Escanes, with other Lords.

HELICANUS
You shall not need, my fellow peers of Tyre,
Further to question me of your king's departure.
His sealed commission left in trust with me
Does speak sufficiently he's gone to travel.
THALIARD, ⌜*aside*⌝   How? The King gone?   15
HELICANUS
If further yet you will be satisfied
Why, as it were, unlicensed of your loves
He would depart, I'll give some light unto you.
Being at Antioch—
THALIARD, ⌜*aside*⌝   What from Antioch?   20
HELICANUS
Royal Antiochus, on what cause I know not,
Took some displeasure at him—at least he judged so;
And doubting lest he had erred or sinned,
To show his sorrow, he'd correct himself;
So puts himself unto the shipman's toil,   25
With whom each minute threatens life or death.
THALIARD, ⌜*aside*⌝   Well, I perceive I shall not be hanged
now, although I would; but since he's gone, the
King's ⌜ears it⌝ must please. He 'scaped the land to
perish at the sea. I'll present myself.—Peace to the   30
lords of Tyre!
⌜HELICANUS⌝
Lord Thaliard from Antiochus is welcome.

35. **betook:** committed
38. **Commended to:** i.e., since it was to be delivered into the keeping of

1.4 In Tarsus, King Cleon, Queen Dionyza, and the citizens of the country, dying of hunger, are saved by Pericles and his shiploads of grain.

---

5. **who:** i.e., he who; **digs:** excavates; **aspire:** mount up, rise high
8. **mischief's eyes:** i.e., the **eyes** of misfortune or distress
9. **being topped:** i.e., **being** pruned (literally, having their tops cut off)
11. **wanteth:** (1) lacks; (2) desires
16. **heaven:** i.e., the gods; **want:** i.e., lack the necessities of life
17. **They:** i.e., **our woes; their helpers:** i.e., the gods (**Helpers** is often emended to "helps." With that emendation, "their helps" would mean "the assistance of **heaven**.")
18. **then:** therefore
19. **wanting breath:** i.e., (1) because you lack **breath;** or (2) when I run out of **breath**

THALIARD   From him I come with message unto princely
  Pericles, but since my landing I have understood
  your lord has ⌜betook⌝ himself to unknown travels.　35
  Now message must return from whence it came.

HELICANUS   We have no reason to desire it,
 Commended to our master, not to us.
 Yet ere you shall depart, this we desire:
 As friends to Antioch, we may feast in Tyre.　40
          ⌜*They*⌝ *exit.*

⌜Scene 4⌝

Enter Cleon the Governor of Tarsus, with his wife
⌜*Dionyza*⌝ *and others.*

CLEON
 My Dionyza, shall we rest us here
 And, by relating tales of others' griefs,
 See if 'twill teach us to forget our own?

DIONYZA
 That were to blow at fire in hope to quench it;
 For who digs hills because they do aspire　5
 Throws down one mountain to cast up a higher.
 O, my distressèd lord, even such our griefs are.
 Here they are but felt, and seen with mischief's eyes,
 But like to groves, being topped, they higher rise.

CLEON   O Dionyza,　10
 Who wanteth food, and will not say he wants it,
 Or can conceal his hunger till he famish?
 Our tongues and sorrows ⌜do⌝ sound deep our woes
 Into the air, our eyes ⌜do⌝ weep till ⌜lungs⌝
 Fetch breath that may proclaim them louder, that　15
 If heaven slumber while their creatures want,
 They may awake their helpers to comfort them.
 I'll then discourse our woes, felt several years,
 And, wanting breath to speak, help me with tears.

22. **on whom Plenty held full hand:** The image is perhaps that of **Plenty** holding an overflowing **hand** over the city. (See picture below.)

23. **her streets:** i.e., the **streets** of Tarsus

27. **jetted:** strutted; **adorned:** i.e., **adorned** themselves

28. **glass:** mirror; **trim them:** i.e., array themselves

32. **name of help:** i.e., the word **help**; **repeat:** mention

34. **by this:** i.e., through the example of

37. **they:** i.e., **earth, sea, and air** (line 35)

38. **for want:** i.e., through lack

39. **They:** i.e., the **mouths** (line 35)

40. **who:** which; **savors:** i.e., meals or tastes (often emended to "summers")

41. **inventions:** i.e., original concoctions

43. **nuzzle up:** nurture

44. **curious:** exquisitely prepared, dainty

Abundance, or Plenty. (1.4.22)
From Cesare Ripa, *Iconologia* . . . (1613).

DIONYZA   I'll do my best, sir.   20

CLEON
  This Tarsus, o'er which I have the government,
  A city on whom Plenty held full hand,
  For Riches strewed herself even in her streets;
  Whose towers bore heads so high they kissed the
    clouds,   25
  And strangers ne'er beheld but wondered at;
  Whose men and dames so jetted and adorned,
  Like one another's glass to trim them by;
  Their tables were stored full to glad the sight,
  And not so much to feed on as delight;   30
  All poverty was scorned, and pride so great,
  The name of help grew odious to repeat.

DIONYZA   O, 'tis too true.

CLEON
  But see what heaven can do by this our change:
  These mouths who but of late earth, sea, and air   35
  Were all too little to content and please,
  Although ⌜they⌝ gave their creatures in abundance,
  As houses are defiled for want of use,
  They are now starved for want of exercise.
  Those palates who not yet two savors younger   40
  Must have inventions to delight the taste,
  Would now be glad of bread and beg for it.
  Those mothers who, to nuzzle up their babes,
  Thought naught too curious, are ready now
  To eat those little darlings whom they loved.   45
  So sharp are hunger's teeth that man and wife
  Draw lots who first shall die to lengthen life.
  Here stands a lord and there a lady weeping;
  Here many sink, yet those which see them fall
  Have scarce strength left to give them burial.   50
  Is not this true?

DIONYZA
  Our cheeks and hollow eyes do witness it.

53. **Plenty's cup:** i.e., the horn of plenty, the cornucopia (symbol of abundance)

54. **largely:** copiously, abundantly

55. **superfluous:** immoderate, inordinate; **riots:** debaucheries; extravagant displays; **tears:** i.e., expressions of grief (This word is sometimes emended to "hearts.")

59. **sorrows . . . bring'st:** confusion of **"sorrows, which** thou **bring'st"** with **"sorrows, which** bring **thee"**

62. **portly sail of ships:** i.e., majestic fleet

68. **power:** fighting forces

70. **unhappy:** unfortunate; distressed

71. **Whereas:** where; **to overcome:** i.e., in conquering

72. **least fear:** i.e., thing we should **fear least**

75. **him's untutored to repeat:** i.e., someone not taught to recite (and therefore who does not understand) that

79. **The ground's the lowest:** Proverbial: "He that lies upon the ground can fall no lower."

80. **attend:** wait for

CLEON
  O, let those cities that of Plenty's cup
  And her prosperities so largely taste,
  With their superfluous riots, hear these tears.   55
  The misery of Tarsus may be theirs.

                    Enter a Lord.

LORD   Where's the Lord Governor?
CLEON   Here.
  Speak out thy sorrows, which thee bring'st in haste,
  For comfort is too far for us to expect.   60
LORD
  We have descried upon our neighboring shore
  A portly sail of ships make hitherward.
CLEON   I thought as much.
  One sorrow never comes but brings an heir
  That may succeed as his inheritor;   65
  And so in ours. Some neighboring nation,
  Taking advantage of our misery,
  ⌜Hath⌝ stuffed the hollow vessels with their power
  To beat us down, the which are down already,
  And make a conquest of unhappy ⌜men,⌝   70
  Whereas no glory's got to overcome.
LORD
  That's the least fear, for, by the semblance
  Of their white flags displayed, they bring us peace
  And come to us as favorers, not as foes.
CLEON
  Thou speak'st like him's untutored to repeat   75
  "Who makes the fairest show means most deceit."
  But bring they what they will and what they can,
  What need we ⌜fear?⌝
  ⌜The⌝ ground's the lowest, and we are halfway there.
  Go tell their general we attend him here,   80
  To know for what he comes and whence he comes
  And what he craves.

84. **consist:** insist
88. **amaze:** terrify, alarm
93. **you happily:** i.e., which you perhaps
94. **Trojan horse:** an enormous wooden **horse, stuffed** with Greek soldiers who burned down Troy (See picture below.)
95. **bloody:** bloodthirsty; **veins:** i.e., warriors; **expecting overthrow:** perhaps, (the warriors) awaiting their **overthrow** of the Trojans; or, perhaps, (**you** [line 93]) awaiting defeat
96. **corn:** grain; **needy:** needful, necessary
103. **gratify:** show gratitude (for); or, recompense (with **love** and **harborage** [lines 101–2])
104. **in thought:** i.e., even **in thought**
106. **succeed:** follow as a consequence of
110. **stars ... smile:** i.e., the bad fortune I am currently suffering turns to good fortune (In astrological belief, the **stars** control one's destiny.)

The Trojan horse. (1.4.94)
From Octavio Boldoni, *Theatrum temporaneum . . .* (1636).

LORD   I go, my lord.   ⌜*He exits.*⌝
CLEON
  Welcome is peace, if he on peace consist;
  If wars, we are unable to resist.   85

    Enter Pericles with Attendants.

PERICLES
  Lord Governor, for so we hear you are,
  Let not our ships and number of our men
  Be like a beacon fired t' amaze your eyes.
  We have heard your miseries as far as Tyre
  And seen the desolation of your streets;   90
  Nor come we to add sorrow to your tears,
  But to relieve them of their heavy load;
  And these our ships, you happily may think
  Are like the Trojan horse was stuffed within
  With bloody veins expecting overthrow,   95
  Are stored with corn to make your needy bread
  And give them life whom hunger starved half dead.
ALL, ⌜*kneeling*⌝
  The gods of Greece protect you, and we'll pray for
    you.
PERICLES   Arise, I pray you, rise.   100
  We do not look for reverence, but for love,
  And harborage for ourself, our ships, and men.
CLEON, ⌜*rising, with the others*⌝
  The which when any shall not gratify
  Or pay you with unthankfulness in thought,
  Be it our wives, our children, or ourselves,   105
  The curse of heaven and men succeed their evils!
  Till when—the which I hope shall ne'er be seen—
  Your Grace is welcome to our town and us.
PERICLES
  Which welcome we'll accept, feast here awhile,
  Until our stars that frown lend us a smile.   110
                                    They exit.

PERICLES,

Prince of Tyre

ACT 2

2 Chorus Gower tells of Pericles' departure from Tarsus and of the storm that destroys his ships and men and tosses him ashore alone.

---

2. **iwis:** indeed (Middle English)

3. **A better:** i.e., (**you have** also **seen** [line 1]) **a better**

4. **awful:** worthy of profound respect

6. **passed necessity:** i.e., gone through difficult times

7. **in troubles reign:** i.e., who **reign** (while) assailed by **troubles** (Some editors punctuate as "in trouble's reign.")

8. **mite:** a minute fragment (Proverbial: "Not worth **a mite**.")

9. **The good:** i.e., Pericles; **conversation:** behavior, conduct

10. **benison:** blessing

12. **Writ:** i.e., holy scripture; **speken can:** is able to speak (an archaic form)

13. **remember:** commemorate

15. **tidings:** happenings, events; news

16 SD. **Dumb Show:** stage action without speech; **all the train with them:** Presumably both Cleon and Pericles are accompanied by a **train** or retinue of attendants. **knights him:** i.e., touches his shoulder with a sword, signaling that he is now a knight

⌈ACT 2⌉

⌈2 Chorus⌉

Enter Gower.

⌈GOWER⌉
Here have you seen a mighty king
His child, iwis, to incest bring;
A better prince and benign lord
That will prove awful both in deed and word.
Be quiet, then, as men should be,   5
Till he hath passed necessity.
I'll show you those in troubles reign,
Losing a mite, a mountain gain.
The good in conversation,
To whom I give my benison,   10
Is still at Tarsus, where each man
Thinks all is Writ he speken can,
And, to remember what he does,
Build his statue to make him glorious.
But tidings to the contrary   15
Are brought your eyes. What need speak I?

Dumb Show.

*Enter at one door Pericles talking with Cleon, all the
train with them. Enter at another door a Gentleman,
with a letter to Pericles. Pericles shows the letter to
Cleon. Pericles gives the Messenger a reward and knights
him. Pericles exits at one door, and Cleon at another.*

43

19. **for though he strive:** The text may be faulty here, and editors often emend. No specific emendation has been generally accepted.

23. **full bent with:** i.e., fully determined to (The image suggests a bow, in archery or battle, **bent** to its limit.)

26. **rest:** residence, abode

27. **doing so:** perhaps, following the letter's advice (Editors often emend.)

28. **been:** an archaic form of *are*

32. **Should:** i.e., which **should**

35. **pelf:** property, possessions

36. **Ne aught escapend:** not anything escaping

37. **Fortune:** i.e., the goddess Fortuna, whose wheel determines one's good or bad luck (See pictures, pages 78 and 172.)

38. **glad:** joy, gladness

40. **'longs:** belongs to

2.1 Fishermen in Pentapolis provide the shipwrecked Pericles with clothing and then pull his armor from the sea. They agree to help him journey to King Simonides' court to take part in a tournament for the king's daughter's birthday.

---

1. **stars of heaven:** i.e., **stars** controlling my fate

4. **my nature:** i.e., as an **earthly man**

Good Helicane, that stayed at home—
Not to eat honey like a drone
From others' labors, for though he strive
To killen bad, keep good alive,   20
And to fulfill his prince' desire—
⌜Sends word⌝ of all that haps in Tyre:
How Thaliard came full bent with sin,
And had intent to murder him;
And that in Tarsus was not best   25
Longer for him to make his rest.
He, doing so, put forth to seas,
Where when men been there's seldom ease;
For now the wind begins to blow;
Thunder above and deeps below   30
Makes such unquiet that the ship
Should house him safe is wracked and split,
And he, good prince, having all lost,
By waves from coast to coast is tossed.
All perishen of man, of pelf,   35
Ne aught escapend but himself;
Till Fortune, tired with doing bad,
Threw him ashore to give him glad.
And here he comes. What shall be next,
Pardon old Gower—this 'longs the text.   40

⌜*He exits.*⌝

⌜Scene 1⌝

Enter Pericles, wet.

PERICLES
Yet cease your ire, you angry stars of heaven!
Wind, rain, and thunder, remember earthly man
Is but a substance that must yield to you,
And I, as fits my nature, do obey you.
Alas, the seas hath cast me on the rocks,   5

6. my breath: i.e., my life (often changed by editors to "me **breath**")

12. Pilch: A **pilch** is a leather or coarse woolen outer garment.

16. Look . . . stirr'st: i.e., "look alive," "get a move on" (literally, see that you bestir yourself)

17. wanion: i.e., vengeance, curse

19. before us: i.e., **before** our eyes

22. welladay: alas

25–26. porpoise . . . tumbled: Such action was thought at the time to predict a major storm.

28. marvel: ask myself, wonder

34. heard on a' the land: i.e., **heard** of on land

". . . the great ones eat up the little ones." (2.1.29–30)
From Geoffrey Whitney, *A choice of emblemes . . .* (1586).

Washed me from shore to shore, and left my breath
Nothing to think on but ensuing death.
Let it suffice the greatness of your powers
To have bereft a prince of all his fortunes;
And, having thrown him from your wat'ry grave,   10
Here to have death in peace is all he'll crave.

Enter three Fishermen.

FIRST FISHERMAN What ⌜ho,⌝ Pilch!
SECOND FISHERMAN Ha, come and bring away the nets!
FIRST FISHERMAN What, Patchbreech, I say!
THIRD FISHERMAN What say you, master?   15
FIRST FISHERMAN Look how thou stirr'st now! Come
    away, or I'll fetch thee with a wanion.
THIRD FISHERMAN Faith, master, I am thinking of the
    poor men that were cast away before us even now.
FIRST FISHERMAN Alas, poor souls, it grieved my heart   20
    to hear what pitiful cries they made to us to help
    them, when, welladay, we could scarce help our-
    selves!
THIRD FISHERMAN Nay, master, said not I as much
    when I saw the porpoise how he bounced and tum-   25
    bled? They say they're half fish, half flesh. A plague
    on them! They ne'er come but I look to be washed.
    Master, I marvel how the fishes live in the sea.
FIRST FISHERMAN Why, as men do a-land: the great
    ones eat up the little ones. I can compare our rich   30
    misers to nothing so fitly as to a whale: he plays
    and tumbles, driving the poor fry before him and
    at last ⌜devours⌝ them all at a mouthful. Such
    whales have I heard on a' the land, who never leave
    gaping till they swallowed the whole parish—   35
    church, steeple, bells and all.
PERICLES, ⌜*aside*⌝ A pretty moral.
THIRD FISHERMAN But, master, if I had been the sexton,
    I would have been that day in the belfry.

44. **left:** ceased, stopped

50. **subject:** i.e., subjects, citizens

52. **recollect:** collect, gather

53. **men approve . . . detect:** i.e., commend **men** or accuse them

55–57. **Honest . . . it:** These lines have never been satisfactorily explained. Editorial repunctuations of the lines have not led to clarity, though the suggestion that **honest** could have been perceived by the fishermen as condescending seems persuasive.

58. **May:** i.e., you **may**

60. **cast thee:** wordplay on (1) throw you; (2) vomit you

A tennis court. (2.1.62)
From Guillaume de La Perrière, *Le théâtre des bons engins* . . . [1539?].

SECOND FISHERMAN   Why, man?   40
⌈THIRD⌉ FISHERMAN   Because he should have swallowed
     me too. And when I had been in his belly, I would
     have kept such a jangling of the bells that he should
     never have left till he cast bells, steeple, church, and
     parish up again. But if the good King Simonides   45
     were of my mind—
PERICLES, ⌈*aside*⌉   Simonides?
THIRD FISHERMAN   We would purge the land of these
     drones that rob the bee of her honey.
PERICLES, ⌈*aside*⌉
  How from the ⌈finny⌉ subject of the sea   50
  These fishers tell the infirmities of men,
  And from their wat'ry empire recollect
  All that may men approve or men detect!—
  Peace be at your labor, honest fishermen.
SECOND FISHERMAN   Honest good fellow, what's that? If   55
     it be a day fits you, search out of the calendar, and
     nobody look after it!
PERICLES
  May see the sea hath cast upon your coast—
SECOND FISHERMAN   What a drunken knave was the sea
     to cast thee in our way!   60
PERICLES
  A man whom both the waters and the wind
  In that vast tennis court hath made the ball
  For them to play upon entreats you pity him.
  He asks of you that never used to beg.
FIRST FISHERMAN   No, friend, cannot you beg? Here's   65
     them in our country of Greece gets more with beg-
     ging than we can do with working.
SECOND FISHERMAN, ⌈*to Pericles*⌉   Canst thou catch any
     fishes, then?
PERICLES   I never practiced it.   70
SECOND FISHERMAN   Nay, then, thou wilt starve sure,
     for here's nothing to be got nowadays unless thou
     canst fish for 't.

76. **thronged up:** filled, crammed **up**

80. **For that:** i.e., because, since

81. **quotha:** i.e., did he say; **an:** if (i.e., so long as, given the fact that)

83–84. **afore me:** a mild oath

97. **beadle:** a parish constable, charged with administering corporal punishment (The implication is that the **beadle** was paid according to how many he whipped.)

99. **becomes:** suits

103–4. **Pentapolis:** The name of this city can be found in both Gower (as "Pentapolim") and in Twine. (For Gower and Twine, see Appendix.) While there were, in antiquity, actual cities and collections of cities called "Pentapolis," scholars do not agree on which is the most likely location for the action in this play. (See longer note, page 191.)

A Fisher Man.

A fisherman. (2.1.11 SD)
From John Speed, *A prospect of the most famous parts of the world . . .* (1631).

PERICLES
What I have been I have forgot to know,
But what I am want teaches me to think on: 75
A man thronged up with cold. My veins are chill
And have no more of life than may suffice
To give my tongue that heat to ask your help—
Which, if you shall refuse, when I am dead,
For that I am a man, pray you see me buried.   80

FIRST FISHERMAN   Die, quotha? Now gods forbid 't, an I
have a gown. Here, come, put it on; keep thee
warm. ⌜*Pericles puts on the garment.*⌝ Now, afore
me, a handsome fellow! Come, thou shalt go home,
and we'll have flesh for ⌜holidays,⌝ fish for fasting   85
days, and, ⌜moreo'er,⌝ puddings and flapjacks, and
thou shalt be welcome.

PERICLES   I thank you, sir.

SECOND FISHERMAN   Hark you, my friend. You said you
could not beg?   90

PERICLES   I did but crave.

SECOND FISHERMAN   But crave? Then I'll turn craver
too, and so I shall 'scape whipping.

PERICLES   Why, are ⌜your⌝ beggars whipped, then?

SECOND FISHERMAN   O, not all, my friend, not all; for if   95
all your beggars were whipped, I would wish no
better office than to be beadle.—But, master, I'll go
draw up the net. ⌜*He exits with Third Fisherman.*⌝

PERICLES, ⌜*aside*⌝
How well this honest mirth becomes their labor!

FIRST FISHERMAN   Hark you, sir, do you know where   100
you are?

PERICLES   Not well.

FIRST FISHERMAN   Why, I'll tell you. This ⌜is⌝ called Pentapolis, and our king the good Simonides.

PERICLES   "The good Simonides" do you call him?   105

FIRST FISHERMAN   Ay, sir, and he deserves so to be called
for his peaceable reign and good government.

108. **happy:** fortunate

111. **Marry:** indeed

117. **make one:** i.e., be one of them, join in

119–20. **what . . . soul:** Editors compare these puzzling words to language in other plays about the selling of wives (or their chastity) as a way to get ahead, or to get (beget) children.

123. **Bots on 't:** i.e., curses on it (The **bots** was a disease caused by a parasitical worm.)

126. **Fortune:** See note to 2 Chor. 37. **yet:** i.e., in spite of (all that you've done to me); **crosses:** afflictions

132. **brace:** part of the armor covering the arms

133. **For that:** i.e., because

136. **kept:** resided, lodged

139. **shipwrack:** shipwreck; **ill:** misfortune

140. **here my:** i.e., **here** that which **my**

"Drawing up a net." (2.1.120 SD)
From Aesop, *Fables d'Esope . . .* (1678).

PERICLES   He is a happy king, since he gains from his
subjects the name of "good" by his government.
How far is his court distant from this shore?   110

FIRST FISHERMAN   Marry, sir, half a day's journey. And
I'll tell you, he hath a fair daughter, and tomorrow
is her birthday; and there are princes and knights
come from all parts of the world to joust and tourney for her love.   115

PERICLES   Were my fortunes equal to my desires, I
could wish to make one there.

FIRST FISHERMAN   O, sir, things must be as they may;
and what a man cannot get he may lawfully deal
for his wife's soul.   120

Enter the two ⌐other¬ Fishermen, drawing up a net.

SECOND FISHERMAN   Help, master, help! Here's a fish
hangs in the net like a poor man's right in the law:
'twill hardly come out. Ha! Bots on 't, 'tis come at
last, and 'tis turned to a rusty armor.

PERICLES
An armor, friends? I pray you let me see it.   125
                              ⌐*They pull out the armor.*¬
Thanks, Fortune, yet, that after all ⌐thy¬ crosses
Thou givest me somewhat to repair myself;
And though it was mine own, part of my heritage
Which my dead father did bequeath to me
With this strict charge even as he left his life,   130
"Keep it, my Pericles; it hath been a shield
'Twixt me and death," and pointed to this brace,
"For that it saved me, keep it. In like necessity—
The which the gods protect thee ⌐from¬—⌐may 't¬
defend thee."   135
It kept where I kept, I so dearly loved it,
Till the rough seas, that spares not any man,
Took it in rage, though calmed have given 't again.
I thank thee for 't; my shipwrack now's no ill
Since I have here my father gave in his will.   140

142. **coat:** i.e., **coat** of mail, armor

143. **sometime target to:** i.e., once protector of (A **target** is literally a light **shield** [line 131]; see picture, page 74.)

149. **pay:** repay; **bounties:** generous acts

151. **virtue:** ability, distinction

152. **do 'ee take:** i.e., **take**

153. **on 't:** i.e., from it, of it

155–56. **made up . . . waters:** In this strange metaphor, the speaker describes their pulling the armor **through the waters** of the sea using language from tailoring (where **made up** means "put together, sewed," and **seams** are stitches holding cloth together).

156–57. **condolements:** perhaps wordplay on "doles" (gifts, charitable handouts)

157. **vails:** tips, gratuities (with wordplay on "leftover scraps of cloth")

158. **them:** i.e., it (the **coat** of armor [line 142])

161. **rupture:** perhaps, breaking of waves (often emended by editors to "rapture"—i.e., plundering)

162. **This jewel . . . arm:** i.e., **This** jeweled bracelet has remained **on my arm.** (See longer note, page 192.)

163–64. **Unto . . . courser:** i.e., I will (obtain and) ride a horse equal to your **value** (The sentence is addressed to the bracelet.)

167. **pair of bases:** i.e., skirts (of cloth or mail) worn below the armor of mounted knights **pair:** used here, as often, to refer to a collective whole (as "pair of beads" for "necklace")

169. **gown:** everyday upper garment worn by men

FIRST FISHERMAN What mean you, sir?

PERICLES
  To beg of you, kind friends, this coat of worth,
  For it was sometime target to a king;
  I know it by this mark. He loved me dearly,
  And for his sake I wish the having of it,   145
  And that you'd guide me to your sovereign's court,
  Where with it I may appear a gentleman.
  And if that ever my low fortune's better,
  I'll pay your bounties; till then, rest your debtor.

FIRST FISHERMAN Why, wilt thou tourney for the lady?   150

PERICLES
  I'll show the virtue I have borne in arms.

FIRST FISHERMAN Why, do 'ee take it, and the gods give
  thee good on 't.

SECOND FISHERMAN Ay, but hark you, my friend, 'twas
  we that made up this garment through the rough   155
  seams of the waters. There are certain condolements, certain vails. I hope, sir, if you thrive, you'll
  remember from whence you had them.

PERICLES Believe 't, I will. ⌜*He puts on the armor.*⌝
  By your furtherance I am clothed in steel,   160
  And spite of all the rupture of the sea,
  This jewel holds his ⌜biding⌝ on my arm.
  Unto thy value I will mount myself
  Upon a courser, whose ⌜delightful⌝ steps
  Shall make the gazer joy to see him tread.   165
  Only, my friend, I yet am unprovided
  Of a pair of bases.

SECOND FISHERMAN We'll sure provide. Thou shalt have
  my best gown to make thee a pair; and I'll bring
  thee to the court myself.   170

PERICLES
  Then honor be but a goal to my will;
  This day I'll rise or else add ill to ill.

  ⌜*They exit.*⌝

2.2 At the court, Pericles and other knights present their shields to Princess Thaisa, and Pericles wins the tournament.

---

1. **triumph:** tournament
3. **stay:** await
4. **Return:** tell, reply to
6. **gat:** begot
12. **jewels:** costly ornaments of precious metals or stones
13. **respected:** (1) treated with esteem; (2) looked upon, regarded
14. **honor:** perhaps, honorable obligation; **entertain:** receive
15. **his device:** the emblematic figure he will present
17. **prefer:** present
21. **word:** motto; **Lux . . . mihi:** Thy life [is] light to me (Latin).

Plus par doulceur, que par force.

An emblem illustrating "More by gentleness than by force." (2.2.27–28)
From Gilles Corrozet, *Hecatongraphie* . . . (1543).

⌜Scene 2⌝

Enter ⌜King⌝ Simonides, with ⌜Lords,⌝ Attendants,
and Thaisa.

SIMONIDES
  Are the knights ready to begin the triumph?
FIRST LORD   They are, my liege,
  And stay your coming to present themselves.
SIMONIDES
  Return them we are ready, and our daughter here,
  In honor of whose birth these triumphs are,   5
  Sits here like Beauty's child, whom Nature gat
  For men to see and, seeing, wonder at.
                              ⌜*An Attendant exits.*⌝

THAISA
  It pleaseth you, my royal father, to express
  My commendations great, whose merit's less.
SIMONIDES
  It's fit it should be so, for princes are   10
  A model which heaven makes like to itself.
  As jewels lose their glory if neglected,
  So princes their renowns if not respected.
  'Tis now your honor, daughter, to entertain
  The labor of each knight in his device.   15
THAISA
  Which to preserve mine honor, I'll perform.

The first Knight passes by. ⌜His Squire presents a shield
to Thaisa.⌝

SIMONIDES
  Who is the first that doth prefer himself?
THAISA
  A knight of Sparta, my renownèd father,
  And the device he bears upon his shield
  Is a black Ethiop reaching at the sun;   20
  The word: *Lux tua vita mihi.*

22. **holds his life of you:** a polite response to the Latin motto (line 21)

27–28. **Pue . . . forsa:** These words are not **Spanish,** as Thaisa claims, but are closer to a garbled Italian. They may mean "More by gentleness than by force." (See picture, page 56.)

31. **chivalry:** knighthood

32. **Me . . . apex:** The desire of renown hath set me forward (as this Latin motto is translated in Claude Paradin's *Heroicall Deuises* [1591]).

35. **Qui . . . extinguit:** He who feeds me extinguishes me (Latin). See picture below.

36. **his:** its

39. **by the touchstone tried:** i.e., been proved genuine **gold** by being **tried** (tested) on a piece of quartz or jasper called a **touchstone** (See picture, page 162.)

40. **Sic spectanda fides:** So should faith be tested (Latin).

The image of "A burning torch . . . turned upside down." (2.2.34)
From Geoffrey Whitney, *A choice of emblems* . . . (1586).

SIMONIDES
  He loves you well that holds his life of you.

  *The second Knight ⌜passes by. His Squire presents a
          shield to Thaisa.⌝*

  Who is the second that presents himself?
THAISA
  A prince of Macedon, my royal father,
  And the device he bears upon his shield   25
  Is an armed knight that's conquered by a lady.
  The motto thus, in Spanish: *Pue per doleera kee per
          forsa.*

  *The third Knight ⌜passes by. His Squire presents a shield
          to Thaisa.⌝*

SIMONIDES   And ⌜what's⌝ the third?
THAISA   The third, of Antioch;   30
  And his device a wreath of chivalry;
  The word: *Me pompae provexit apex.*

  *The fourth Knight ⌜passes by. His Squire presents a
          shield to Thaisa.⌝*

SIMONIDES   What is the fourth?
THAISA
  A burning torch that's turnèd upside down;
  The word: *Qui me alit me extinguit.*   35
SIMONIDES
  Which shows that beauty hath his power and will,
  Which can as well inflame as it can kill.

  *The fifth Knight ⌜passes by. His Squire presents a shield
          to Thaisa.⌝*

THAISA
  The fifth, an hand environèd with clouds,
  Holding out gold that's by the touchstone tried;
  The motto thus: *Sic spectanda fides.*   40

43. **courtesy:** bow

44. **his present:** i.e., that which he presents (presumably a shield with the **branch** [line 45] emblazoned on it)

46. **In hac spe vivo:** In this hope I live (Latin).

50. **had need:** i.e., must of necessity

51. **commend:** commendation

53. **whipstock:** stick to which the lash of a whip is attached (used by such menials as cart drivers)

55. **strangely furnishèd:** oddly dressed or equipped (with wordplay on **stranger** as foreigner [line 54])

56. **on set purpose:** deliberately, intentionally

58. **scan:** judge; perceive, discern

59. **The . . . man:** The words **outward** and **inward** are apparently reversed. (The Folger Library owns a book in which is written, in a 17th-century hand, "he is **a foole** that scans **the Inward** habits **by the outwarde man.** Shakesphere.") **habit:** garment (See longer note, page 192.)

60. **stay:** wait

61 SD. **mean:** undistinguished, poor

*The sixth Knight, ⌈Pericles, passes by. He presents a
shield to Thaisa.⌉*

SIMONIDES
  And what's the sixth and last, the which the knight
    himself
  With such a graceful courtesy delivered?
THAISA
  He seems to be a stranger; but his present is
  A withered branch that's only green at top,   45
  The motto: *In hac spe vivo.*
SIMONIDES   A pretty moral.
  From the dejected state wherein he is,
  He hopes by you his fortunes yet may flourish.
FIRST LORD
  He had need mean better than his outward show   50
  Can any way speak in his just commend,
  For by his rusty outside he appears
  To have practiced more the whipstock than the lance.
SECOND LORD
  He well may be a stranger, for he comes
  To an honored triumph strangely furnishèd.   55
THIRD LORD
  And on set purpose let his armor rust
  Until this day, to scour it in the dust.
SIMONIDES
  Opinion's but a fool that makes us scan
  The outward habit by the inward man.
  But stay, the knights are coming.   60
  We will withdraw into the gallery.
                                        ⌈*They exit.*⌉

Great shouts ⌈offstage,⌉ and all cry, "The mean knight."

2.3 Simonides and Thaisa separately express their admiration for "the stranger knight."

---

3. **volume of your deeds:** i.e., book recording **your deeds** (The **title page** of a book [line 4] often praised the **worth** of its contents. See picture below.)

7. **becomes:** is appropriate to

14. **envies:** resents

17. **her labored scholar:** i.e., student over whom **Art** has **labored** (and made **to exceed** [line 16])

20. **Marshal, the rest as:** i.e., **Marshal,** (seat) **the rest** (in the order) that; **their grace:** i.e., the favor conferred upon them

22. **glads:** gladdens

23. **who:** i.e., whoever

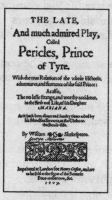

Title page of the 1609 *Pericles* Quarto.
(From George Steevens's copy in the Folger Library Collection.)

⌜Scene 3⌝

Enter the King ⌜*Simonides, Thaisa, Marshal, Ladies,*
Lords, Attendants,⌝ *and Knights* ⌜*in armor,*⌝ *from tilting.*

SIMONIDES Knights,
　To say you're welcome were superfluous.
　⌜To⌝ place upon the volume of your deeds,
　As in a title page, your worth in arms
　Were more than you expect or more than 's fit,　　　5
　Since every worth in show commends itself.
　Prepare for mirth, for mirth becomes a feast.
　You are princes and my guests.
THAISA, ⌜*to Pericles*⌝ But you my knight and guest,
　To whom this wreath of victory I give　　　　10
　And crown you king of this day's happiness.
　　　　　⌜*She places a wreath on Pericles' head.*⌝

PERICLES
　'Tis more by fortune, lady, than my merit.

SIMONIDES
　Call it by what you will, the day is ⌜yours,⌝
　And here, I hope, is none that envies it.
　In framing an artist, Art hath thus decreed,　　　15
　To make some good but others to exceed,
　And you are her labored scholar.—Come, queen o'
　　the feast,
　For, daughter, so you are; here, take your place.—
　Marshal, the rest as they deserve their grace.　　　20

KNIGHTS
　We are honored much by good Simonides.

SIMONIDES
　Your presence glads our days. Honor we love,
　For who hates honor hates the gods above.
MARSHAL, ⌜*to Pericles*⌝ Sir, yonder is your place.
PERICLES Some other is more fit.　　　　25

FIRST KNIGHT
　Contend not, sir, for we are gentlemen

27. **Have:** who **have**

28. **Envies:** i.e., anything that **envies**

31. **By . . . thoughts:** i.e., **By Jove, who is king of thoughts, I** marvel (that)

32. **cates:** delicacies; **resist:** repel

33. **Juno:** wife of **Jove**

34. **unsavory:** tasteless, insipid

35. **meat:** food

39. **broken a staff or so:** i.e., contended with a few antagonists; or, perhaps, shattered a few lances

40. **to:** as compared with

42. **tells:** proclaims (that) (Many editions add "me" after **tells.**)

46. **vail their crowns:** i.e., bow down their crowned heads; or, perhaps, remove **their crowns** (as a sign of submission)

48. **fire:** luminosity

49. **Time's the king of men:** See picture, page 184.

53. **other:** anything else

54. **stored:** i.e., filled (literally, furnished, supplied)

55. **do you:** i.e., **you do** (The words are printed as "**you do**" in Q4.)

Have neither in our hearts nor outward eyes
Envies the great, nor shall the low despise.

PERICLES
You are right courteous knights.

SIMONIDES   Sit, sir, sit. ⌜*They sit.*⌝   30
⌜*Aside.*⌝ By Jove I wonder, that is king of thoughts,
These cates resist me, he not thought upon.

THAISA, ⌜*aside*⌝
By Juno, that is queen of marriage,
All viands that I eat do seem unsavory,
Wishing him my meat.—Sure, he's a gallant   35
  gentleman.

SIMONIDES
He's but a country gentleman;
Has done no more than other knights have done;
Has broken a staff or so. So let it pass.

THAISA, ⌜*aside*⌝
To me he seems like diamond to glass.   40

PERICLES, ⌜*aside*⌝
⌜Yon⌝ king's to me like to my father's picture,
Which tells in that glory once he was—
Had princes sit like stars about his throne,
And he the sun for them to reverence.
None that beheld him but like lesser lights   45
Did vail their crowns to his supremacy;
Where now his ⌜son's⌝ like a glowworm in the night,
The which hath fire in darkness, none in light;
Whereby I see that Time's the king of men.
He's both their parent, and he is their grave,   50
And gives them what he will, not what they crave.

SIMONIDES   What, are you merry, knights?

KNIGHTS
Who can be other in this royal presence?

SIMONIDES
Here, with a cup that's ⌜stored⌝ unto the brim,
As do you love, fill to your mistress' lips.   55

56. **health:** toast

60. **might countervail:** i.e., that can equal, match, come up to

63. **attend:** pay attention, listen

66–67. **gnats . . . wondered at:** Perhaps the dead **gnats** create amazement because their insignificant size is in such contrast with their previous noisiness.

69. **standing-bowl:** vessel with a stem and base on which to stand

75. **or you'll move me else:** i.e., **or else you'll** make **me** angry

77. **of him:** i.e., from him (Editors frequently cut words or parts of words from this line to improve the meter.)

The three Graces. (1.1.14)
From Vincenzo Cartari, *Le vere e noue imagini . . .* (1615).

We drink this health to you.   ⌜*He drinks.*⌝
KNIGHTS   We thank your Grace.
SIMONIDES
  Yet pause awhile. Yon knight doth sit too melancholy,
  As if the entertainment in our court
  Had not a show might countervail his worth.—   60
  Note it not you, Thaisa?
THAISA   What is 't to me, my father?
SIMONIDES
  O, attend, my daughter. Princes in this
  Should live like gods above, who freely give
  To everyone that come to honor them.   65
  And princes not doing so are like to gnats,
  Which make a sound but, killed, are wondered at.
  Therefore, to make his entrance more sweet,
  Here, say we drink this standing-bowl of wine to him.
                    ⌜*He drinks.*⌝
THAISA
  Alas, my father, it befits not me   70
  Unto a stranger knight to be so bold.
  He may my proffer take for an offense,
  Since men take women's gifts for impudence.
SIMONIDES   How?
  Do as I bid you, or you'll move me else.   75
THAISA, ⌜*aside*⌝
  Now, by the gods, he could not please me better.
SIMONIDES
  And furthermore tell him we desire to know of him
  Of whence he is, his name and parentage.
THAISA, ⌜*going to Pericles*⌝
  The King, my father, sir, has drunk to you.
PERICLES   I thank him.   80
THAISA
  Wishing it so much blood unto your life.
PERICLES
  I thank both him and you, and pledge him freely.
                    ⌜*He drinks to Simonides.*⌝

86. **been:** is (a form of *to be* used consistently by John Gower); **arts:** branches of knowledge often called the "liberal **arts**"

88. **reft:** robbed, forcibly deprived

98. **addressed:** arrayed, attired

99. **become:** suit

102. **in arms:** wordplay on "in armor" and "in their **arms**"

102 SD. **They dance:** This may be a dance of the knights in armor only, or a mixed dance.

103. **So . . . well performed:** perhaps, just as I did **well** in inviting you to dance, **so** you **performed well** in the dance

105. **breathing:** exercise

107. **trip:** wordplay on (1) dance nimbly; (2) fall (i.e., sin)

108. **measures:** grave or stately dances

110–11. **that's . . . courtesy:** In this contorted sentence, Simonides dismisses Pericles' suggestion that he is unpracticed as a dancer.

111 SD. **They dance:** Editors are divided about whether this is a dance of knights and ladies generally or only of Pericles and Thaisa.

THAISA
  And further, he desires to know of you
  Of whence you are, your name and parentage.

PERICLES
  A gentleman of Tyre, my name Pericles.   85
  My education been in arts and arms,
  Who, looking for adventures in the world,
  Was by the rough seas reft of ships and men,
  And after shipwrack driven upon this shore.

THAISA, ⌜*returning to her place*⌝
  He thanks your Grace; names himself Pericles,   90
  A gentleman of Tyre,
  Who only by misfortune of the seas,
  Bereft of ships and men, cast on this shore.

SIMONIDES
  Now, by the gods, I pity his misfortune,
  And will awake him from his melancholy.—   95
  Come, gentlemen, we sit too long on trifles
  And waste the time which looks for other revels.
  Even in your armors, as you are addressed,
  Will well become a soldiers' dance.
  I will not have excuse with saying this: 100
  "Loud music is too harsh for ladies' heads,"
  Since they love men in arms as well as beds.
                                    They dance.
  So, this was well asked, 'twas so well performed.
  Come, sir.   ⌜*He presents Pericles to Thaisa.*⌝
  Here's a lady that wants breathing too,   105
  And I have heard you knights of Tyre
  Are excellent in making ladies trip,
  And that their measures are as excellent.

PERICLES
  In those that practice them they are, my lord.

SIMONIDES
  O, that's as much as you would be denied   110
  Of your fair courtesy.   *They dance.*
                  Unclasp, unclasp!

116. **several:** separate
121. **level:** aim (See picture, page 20.)
123. **speeding:** succeeding

2.4 In Tyre, Helicanus recounts the awful deaths of Antiochus and his daughter. He then agrees to accept the crown twelve months hence if Pericles has not returned. Tyrian lords set out to search for Pericles.

---

3. **minding:** inclining, wishing
10. **for they so stunk:** In this account, Shakespeare conflates the historical **Antiochus** the Great (who appears in Gower) with his descendant, **Antiochus** Epiphanes (from 2 Maccabees). See longer note, page 193.
11. **adored:** i.e., which **adored**
14. **great:** i.e., prominently placed, of high rank
16. **his:** its

The dragon guarding the "golden fruit" of
the Hesperides. (1.1.28–30)
From *Le dodichi fatiche d'Hercole* . . . [ca. 1600].

Thanks, gentlemen, to all; all have done well;
⌜*To Pericles.*⌝ But you the best.—Pages and lights, to
   conduct   115
These knights unto their several lodgings. ⌜*To*
   Pericles.⌝ Yours, sir,
We have given order be next our own.
PERICLES   I am at your Grace's pleasure.
⌜SIMONIDES⌝
Princes, it is too late to talk of love,   120
And that's the mark I know you level at.
Therefore each one betake him to his rest,
Tomorrow all for speeding do their best.
                              ⌜*They exit.*⌝

⌜Scene 4⌝

Enter Helicanus and Escanes.

HELICANUS
No, Escanes, know this of me:
Antiochus from incest lived not free,
For which the most high gods not minding longer
To withhold the vengeance that they had in store
Due to this heinous capital offense,   5
Even in the height and pride of all his glory,
When he was seated in a chariot of
An inestimable value, and his daughter with him,
A fire from heaven came and shriveled up
Those bodies even to loathing, for they so stunk   10
That all those eyes adored them, ere their fall,
Scorn now their hand should give them burial.
ESCANES   'Twas very strange.
HELICANUS
And yet but justice; for though this king were great,
His greatness was no guard to bar heaven's shaft,   15
But sin had his reward.

20. **grieve:** cause offense, vex
24. **griefs:** grievances, injuries
29. **salute:** pay our respects to, visit
33. **resolved:** convinced, satisfied; certain
36. **the strongest . . . censure:** i.e., most likely in our judgment   **censure:** opinion, judgment
38. **Like:** as; **goodly:** splendid, excellent

"Death remembered." (1.1.46–47)
From Richard Turnbull, *An exposition vpon . . .
Saint Jude . . .* (1606).

ESCANES   'Tis very true.

Enter two or three Lords.

FIRST LORD
See, not a man in private conference
Or counsel has respect with him but he.
SECOND LORD
It shall no longer grieve without reproof.   20
THIRD LORD
And cursed be he that will not second it.
FIRST LORD
Follow me, then.—Lord Helicane, a word.
HELICANUS
With me? And welcome. Happy day, my lords.
FIRST LORD
Know that our griefs are risen to the top,
And now at length they overflow their banks.   25
HELICANUS
Your griefs? For what? Wrong not your prince you
love.
FIRST LORD
Wrong not yourself, then, noble Helicane.
But if the Prince do live, let us salute him,
Or know what ground's made happy by his breath.   30
If in the world he live, we'll seek him out;
If in his grave he rest, we'll find him there,
And be resolved he lives to govern us,
Or dead, give 's cause to mourn his funeral
And leave us to our free election.   35
SECOND LORD
Whose ⌜death's⌝ indeed the strongest in our censure;
And knowing this kingdom is without a head—
Like goodly buildings left without a roof
Soon fall to ruin—your noble self,
That best know how to rule and how to reign,   40
We thus submit unto, our sovereign.

43. **Try honor's cause:** perhaps, attempt to act honorably; **forbear:** refrain from urging, dispense with; **suffrages:** expressions of favor (toward me); or, perhaps, votes

44. **forbear:** cease

45. **Take . . . wish:** i.e., if **I** follow **your** wishes

46. **Where's:** i.e., where there is

48. **forbear:** endure, bear

58. **travels:** This word encompasses both the "journeys" and the "travails"—i.e., labors—of their coming search.

2.5 King Simonides, learning that Thaisa loves Pericles, pretends to be angry, but then reveals his pleasure at their mutual love.

---

4. **to . . . known:** i.e., **known only to herself**

A "target" or shield. (2.1.143)
From Louis de Gaya, *A treatise of the arms* . . . (1678).

ALL Live, noble Helicane!
HELICANUS
  Try honor's cause; forbear your suffrages.
  If that you love Prince Pericles, forbear.
  Take I your wish, I leap into the seas,   45
  Where's hourly trouble for a minute's ease.
  A twelve-month longer let me entreat you
  To forbear the absence of your king;
  If in which time expired, he not return,
  I shall with agèd patience bear your yoke.   50
  But if I cannot win you to this love,
  Go search like nobles, like noble subjects,
  And in your search spend your adventurous worth,
  Whom if you find and win unto return,
  You shall like diamonds sit about his crown.   55

FIRST LORD
  To wisdom he's a fool that will not yield.
  And since Lord Helicane enjoineth us,
  We with our travels will endeavor.

HELICANUS
  Then you love us, we you, and we'll clasp hands.
  When peers thus knit, a kingdom ever stands.   60
                                        ⌜*They exit.*⌝

                        ⌜Scene 5⌝

Enter the King, ⌜Simonides,⌝ reading of a letter at one
door; the Knights meet him.

FIRST KNIGHT
  Good morrow to the good Simonides.
SIMONIDES
  Knights, from my daughter this I let you know,
  That for this twelvemonth she'll not undertake
  A married life. Her reason to herself is only known,
  Which from her by no means can I get.   5

9. **wear Diana's livery:** i.e., remain in the service of Diana, goddess of virginity

10. **Cynthia:** Diana in her role of moon goddess (See picture below and page 178.)

14. **dispatched:** disposed of

16. **nor day:** i.e., neither **day**

18. **absolute:** perfectly certain, decided

21. **Soft:** i.e., wait a minute

24. **beholding:** under obligation, beholden

Diana as Cynthia. (2.5.10.)
From Vincenzo Cartari, *Le vere e noue imagini* . . . (1615).

SECOND KNIGHT
  May we not get access to her, my lord?
SIMONIDES
  Faith, by no means; she hath so strictly tied her
  To her chamber that 'tis impossible.
  One twelve moons more she'll wear Diana's livery.
  This by the eye of Cynthia hath she vowed,   10
  And on her virgin honor will not break it.
THIRD KNIGHT
  Loath to bid farewell, we take our leaves.
                              ⌜*The Knights exit.*⌝
SIMONIDES So,
  They are well dispatched. Now to my daughter's letter.
  She tells me here she'll wed the stranger knight   15
  Or never more to view nor day nor light.
  'Tis well, mistress, your choice agrees with mine.
  I like that well. Nay, how absolute she's in 't,
  Not minding whether I dislike or no!
  Well, I do commend her choice, and will no longer   20
  Have it be delayed. Soft, here he comes.
  I must dissemble it.

                      Enter Pericles.

PERICLES
  All fortune to the good Simonides.
SIMONIDES
  To you as much. Sir, I am beholding to you
  For your sweet music this last night. I do   25
  Protest, my ears were never better fed
  With such delightful pleasing harmony.
PERICLES
  It is your Grace's pleasure to commend,
  Not my desert.
SIMONIDES   Sir, you are music's master.   30
PERICLES
  The worst of all her scholars, my good lord.

38. **you must be:** i.e., (she insists that) **you be**

39. **look to it:** i.e., attend **to it,** take care of **it**

41. **else:** i.e., if you don't believe it

44. **subtlety:** trick, stratagem

48. **bent all offices:** i.e., directed **all** my services or attentions

52. **levy:** i.e., undertake (a meaning of **levy** usually restricted to the levying of war)

54. **might:** i.e., which **might**

58–59. **Even . . . lie:** i.e., to anyone who **calls me traitor, unless it be the King,** I say "you lie in your throat" (i.e., you are a complete liar)

Fortune and her wheel. (2 Chor. 37; 2.1.126; 3 Chor. 46; 3.2.64; 4.4.49)
From [John Lydgate,] *The hystorye . . . of Troye* [1513].

SIMONIDES   Let me ask you one thing:
  What do you think of my daughter, sir?
PERICLES   A most virtuous princess.
SIMONIDES   And she is fair too, is she not?   35
PERICLES
  As a fair day in summer, wondrous fair.
SIMONIDES
  Sir, my daughter thinks very well of you,
  Ay, so well that you must be her master,
  And she will be your scholar. Therefore, look to it.
PERICLES
  I am unworthy for her schoolmaster.   40
SIMONIDES
  She thinks not so. Peruse this writing else.
PERICLES, ⌜*aside*⌝   What's here?
  A letter that she loves the knight of Tyre?
  'Tis the King's subtlety to have my life.—
  O, seek not to entrap me, gracious lord,   45
  A stranger and distressèd gentleman
  That never aimed so high to love your daughter,
  But bent all offices to honor her.
SIMONIDES
  Thou hast bewitched my daughter, and thou art
  A villain.   50
PERICLES   By the gods, I have not!
  Never did thought of mine levy offense;
  Nor never did my actions yet commence
  A deed might gain her love or your displeasure.
SIMONIDES
  Traitor, thou liest!   55
PERICLES   Traitor?
SIMONIDES   Ay, traitor.
PERICLES
  Even in his throat, unless it be the King
  That calls me traitor, I return the lie.

62. **relished:** savored, had a touch or trace; **base:** wordplay on (1) of the lower social orders, and (2) morally despicable, suggesting that **noble** (line 61) has a comparable double meaning

64. **her:** i.e., **honor's**

70. **Resolve:** i.e., inform, tell

72. **made love to:** wooed, courted

74. **that would:** i.e., **that** which **would**

75. **peremptory:** decisive, determined

82. **great in blood:** i.e., nobly descended

83. **frame:** conform, adapt

Two knights jousting in a tournament. (2.1.114–15)
From Amadis de Gaule, *Le second livre d'Amadis de Gaule . . .* (1555).

SIMONIDES, ⌈*aside*⌉
  Now, by the gods, I do applaud his courage.   60

PERICLES
  My actions are as noble as my thoughts,
  That never relished of a base descent.
  I came unto your court for honor's cause,
  And not to be a rebel to her state,
  And he that otherwise accounts of me,   65
  This sword shall prove he's honor's enemy.

SIMONIDES No?
  Here comes my daughter. She can witness it.

Enter Thaisa.

PERICLES
  Then as you are as virtuous as fair,
  Resolve your angry father if my tongue   70
  Did e'er solicit or my hand subscribe
  To any syllable that made love to you.

THAISA
  Why, sir, say if you had, who takes offense
  At that would make me glad?

SIMONIDES
  Yea, mistress, are you so peremptory?   75
  (*Aside.*) I am glad on 't with all my heart.—
  I'll tame you! I'll bring you in subjection.
  Will you, not having my consent,
  Bestow your love and your affections
  Upon a stranger? (*Aside.*) Who, for aught I know,   80
  May be—nor can I think the contrary—
  As great in blood as I myself.—
  Therefore, hear you, mistress: either frame
  Your will to mine—and you, sir, hear you:
  Either be ruled by me—or I'll make you   85
  Man and wife.
  Nay, come, your hands and lips must seal it too.
  And being joined, I'll thus your hopes destroy.

Hymen, the god of marriage. (3 Chor. 9)
From Vincenzo Cartari, *Imagines deorum . . .* (1581).

And for further grief—God give you joy!
What, are you both pleased?   90
THAISA   Yes, (⌜*to Pericles*⌝) if you love me, sir.
PERICLES
  Even as my life my blood that fosters it.
SIMONIDES   What, are you both agreed?
BOTH   Yes, if 't please your Majesty.
SIMONIDES
  It pleaseth me so well that I will see you wed,   95
  And then with what haste you can, get you to bed.
                                                    They exit.

PERICLES,

Prince of Tyre

ACT 3

3 Chorus Gower picks up the story on the night after Pericles and Thaisa's wedding and carries it forward through Thaisa's becoming pregnant, the arrival of news that Pericles is needed in Tyre, the embarking of Pericles and his pregnant wife, and the beginning of a terrible storm at sea.

---

1. **yslackèd hath the rout:** i.e., has quieted the company (*To slack* is to make less active.)

4. **pompous:** magnificent

5. **eyne:** eyes (archaic form)

6. **couches from:** lies down at a distance from

7. **sing:** i.e., which **sing**

8. **blither for their drouth:** i.e., happier for being dry

9. **Hymen:** god of marriage (See picture, page 82.)

11. **attent:** attentive

13. **fancies:** imaginations; **quaintly eche:** skillfully augment or increase

14. **plain:** perhaps, make plain, explain, make clear

14 SD. **with child:** i.e., pregnant; **a nurse:** i.e., Thaisa's **nurse** or attendant; **shows her:** i.e., **shows Thaisa**

⌈ACT 3⌉

Enter Gower.

⌈GOWER⌉
Now sleep yslackèd hath the rout;
No din but snores about the house,
Made louder by the o'erfed breast
Of this most pompous marriage feast.
The cat with eyne of burning coal   5
Now couches from the mouse's hole,
And ⌈crickets⌉ sing at the oven's mouth
Are the blither for their drouth.
Hymen hath brought the bride to bed,
Where, by the loss of maidenhead,   10
A babe is molded. Be attent,
And time that is so briefly spent
With your fine fancies quaintly eche.
What's dumb in show I'll plain with speech.

⌈*Dumb Show.*⌉

*Enter Pericles and Simonides at one door with
Attendants. A Messenger meets them, kneels, and gives
Pericles a letter. Pericles shows it Simonides. The Lords
kneel to him; then enter Thaisa with child, with
Lychorida, a nurse. The King shows her the letter. She
rejoices. She and Pericles take leave of her father, and
depart* ⌈*with Lychorida and their Attendants. Then
Simonides and the others exit.*⌉

15. **By . . . perch:** i.e., through **many a** weary mile **dern:** secret; dire **perch:** literally, a measure of roughly five and a half yards

17. **coigns:** corners (The phrase "to **the four** [corners] of **the world**" meant "through the entire **world.**" It is possible that the line should begin with "To" rather than "**By.**")

21. **stead:** be of use to

22. **Fame . . . enquire:** perhaps, rumor responding to far-flung inquiry **strange:** foreign, alien; outside one's own land

28. **will none:** i.e., wants **none** of it

29. **t' oppress:** to crush

30. **Says:** i.e., and he **says**; or, by saying

31. **moons:** months

32. **dooms:** judgments

33. **sum:** gist

35. **Y-ravishèd:** enraptured

36. **can sound:** did proclaim, began to declare

39. **Brief:** i.e., in **brief,** in short

41. **cross:** thwart, oppose

45. **Neptune's billow:** i.e., the sea (Neptune was the Roman god of the sea.)

45–46. **Half . . . cut:** i.e., their vessel had sailed halfway over the waters

46. **Fortune:** See note to 2 Chor. 37. **moved:** angry, disturbed

47. **grizzled:** gray (with possible wordplay on *grisly*)

By many a dern and painful perch   15
Of Pericles the careful search,
By the four opposing coigns
Which the world together joins,
Is made with all due diligence
That horse and sail and high expense   20
Can stead the quest. At last from Tyre,
Fame answering the most strange enquire,
To th' court of King Simonides
Are letters brought, the tenor these:
Antiochus and his daughter dead,   25
The men of Tyrus on the head
Of Helicanus would set on
The crown of Tyre, but he will none.
The mutiny he there hastes t' oppress,
Says to 'em, if King Pericles   30
Come not home in twice six moons,
He, obedient to their dooms,
Will take the crown. The sum of this,
Brought hither to Pentapolis,
Y-ravishèd the regions round,   35
And everyone with claps can sound,
"Our heir apparent is a king!
Who dreamt, who thought of such a thing?"
Brief, he must hence depart to Tyre.
His queen, with child, makes her desire—   40
Which who shall cross?—along to go.
Omit we all their dole and woe.
Lychorida, her nurse, she takes,
And so to sea. Their vessel shakes
On Neptune's billow. Half the flood   45
Hath their keel cut. But Fortune, moved,
Varies again. The grizzled North
Disgorges such a tempest forth
That, as a duck for life that dives,
So up and down the poor ship drives.   50

51. **well-anear:** alas
52. **in travail:** into labor
53. **fell:** cruel, pitiless
55. **nill:** i.e., will not
57. **might not:** i.e., (**action** [line 55]) is not able (to **convey**)
58. **hold:** consider, believe
60. **to speak:** i.e., and speaks

3.1 In the storm, Thaisa dies in giving birth and her body is cast into the sea. To save the baby, Pericles orders the ship to change course and sail to Tarsus.

1–6. **The god . . . flashes:** Pericles seems to call first on Neptune, **god** of the sea, then on Aeolus, **god** of **the winds,** and finally on Jove, **god** of thunder. (See picture, page 24.) **vast:** i.e., ocean
9. **of death:** i.e., of someone who is dead
10. **Lucina:** Roman goddess who presided over childbirth (See picture, page 96.)
16. **conceit:** apprehension, understanding

The lady shrieks and, well-anear,
Does fall in travail with her fear.
And what ensues in this fell storm
Shall for itself itself perform.
I nill relate; action may   55
Conveniently the rest convey,
Which might not what by me is told.
In your imagination hold
This stage the ship upon whose deck
The ⌈sea-tossed⌉ Pericles appears to speak.   60

⌈He exits.⌉

⌈Scene 1⌉

Enter Pericles, a-shipboard.

PERICLES
The god of this great vast, rebuke these surges,
Which wash both heaven and hell! And thou that hast
Upon the winds command, bind them in brass,
Having called them from the deep! O, still
Thy deaf'ning dreadful thunders, gently quench   5
Thy nimble sulfurous flashes.—O, how, Lychorida,
How does my queen?—Then, storm, venomously
Wilt thou spit all thyself? The seaman's whistle
Is as a whisper in the ears of death,
Unheard.—Lychorida!—Lucina, O   10
Divinest patroness and ⌈midwife⌉ gentle
To those that cry by night, convey thy deity
Aboard our dancing boat, make swift the pangs
Of my queen's travails!—Now, Lychorida!

Enter Lychorida, ⌈carrying an infant.⌉

LYCHORIDA
Here is a thing too young for such a place,   15
Who, if it had conceit, would die, as I

17. **like:** i.e., likely

19. **How:** i.e., what

25. **goodly:** splendid, excellent

26. **straight:** immediately

27. **Recall not:** do not take back; **therein:** in that matter

28. **Use:** practice

30. **for:** i.e., for the sake of

32. **blusterous:** rough, stormy

33. **thy conditions:** i.e., (**may be** [line 31]) your circumstances

34. **rudeliest welcome:** i.e., most violently welcomed

35. **Happy what follows:** i.e., may **what follows** be fortunate

40. **Thy . . . here:** i.e., be requited by your natural gifts (**thy portage**) and by your fortune **here** (**Portage** could mean "that which is carried or transported," and "that which a sailor could place aboard when a voyage began.")

41. **best eyes:** i.e., most auspicious looks or influence

43. **flaw:** wind blast

47. **wilt not:** i.e., will not **be quiet** (line 46)

Am like to do. Take in your arms this piece
Of your dead queen.
PERICLES   How? How, Lychorida?
LYCHORIDA
  Patience, good sir. Do not assist the storm.   20
  Here's all that is left living of your queen,
  A little daughter. For the sake of it,
  Be manly and take comfort.
PERICLES   O you gods!
  Why do you make us love your goodly gifts   25
  And snatch them straight away? We here below
  Recall not what we give, and therein may
  Use honor with you.
LYCHORIDA.   Patience, good sir,
  Even for this charge.   ⌜*She hands him the infant.*⌝ 30
PERICLES, ⌜*to the infant*⌝ Now mild may be thy life,
  For a more blusterous birth had never babe.
  Quiet and gentle thy conditions, for
  Thou art the rudeliest welcome to this world
  That ever was prince's child. Happy what follows!   35
  Thou hast as chiding a nativity
  As fire, air, water, earth, and heaven can make
  To herald thee from the womb.
  Even at the first, thy loss is more than can
  Thy portage quit, with all thou canst find here.   40
  Now the good gods throw their best eyes upon 't.

              Enter two Sailors.

FIRST SAILOR   What courage, sir? God save you.
PERICLES
  Courage enough. I do not fear the flaw.
  It hath done to me the worst. Yet for the love
  Of this poor infant, this fresh new seafarer,   45
  I would it would be quiet.
FIRST SAILOR   Slack the bowlines there!—Thou wilt not,
    wilt thou? Blow, and split thyself!

49. **But searoom:** i.e., (so long as we have) room to maneuver; **an:** even if

49–50. **brine and cloudy billow:** i.e., seawater and spray

52. **lie:** become still, subside

56. **still observed:** always adhered to

57. **briefly:** i.e., quickly

58. **straight:** immediately

59. **meet:** fitting, appropriate

60. **Here she lies:** Thaisa's body may be revealed by drawing a curtain, or it may be brought on at this point by sailors.

64. **give thee hallowed to thy grave:** i.e., have you ceremonially buried; or, perhaps, bury you in **hallowed** ground

66. **for a monument:** i.e., in the place of **a monument**

67. **e'er-remaining lamps:** i.e., (in the place of) always abiding lights; **belching:** i.e., spouting

71. **casket:** small ornamental chest

72. **coffin:** i.e., coffer (See longer note, page 194.)

73. **Hie thee:** hurry

74. **Suddenly:** at once

76. **bitumed:** spread (and thus sealed) with pitch

79. **gentle:** a complimentary epithet

80. **for Tyre:** i.e., (which is currently) **for Tyre; reach it:** i.e., **reach** Tarsus

SECOND SAILOR But searoom, an the brine and cloudy
    billow kiss the moon, I care not.   50
FIRST SAILOR Sir, your queen must overboard. The sea
    works high, the wind is loud, and will not lie till
    the ship be cleared of the dead.
PERICLES That's your superstition.
FIRST SAILOR Pardon us, sir; with us at sea it hath been   55
    still observed, and we are strong in ⌐custom.⌐
    Therefore briefly yield 'er, ⌐for she must overboard
    straight.⌐
PERICLES As you think meet.—Most wretched queen!
LYCHORIDA Here she lies, sir.   60
PERICLES
A terrible childbed hast thou had, my dear,
No light, no fire. Th' unfriendly elements
Forgot thee utterly. Nor have I time
To give thee hallowed to thy grave, but straight
Must cast thee, scarcely coffined, in ⌐the ooze,⌐   65
Where, for a monument upon thy bones
⌐And e'er-remaining⌐ lamps, the belching whale
And humming water must o'erwhelm thy corpse,
Lying with simple shells.—O, Lychorida,
Bid Nestor bring me spices, ink, and ⌐paper,⌐   70
My casket and my jewels; and bid Nicander
Bring me the satin coffin. Lay the babe
Upon the pillow. Hie thee, whiles I say
A priestly farewell to her. Suddenly, woman!
                     ⌐*Lychorida exits.*⌐
SECOND SAILOR Sir, we have a chest beneath the hatches,   75
    caulked and bitumed ready.
PERICLES
I thank thee, mariner. Say, what coast is this?
SECOND SAILOR We are near Tarsus.
PERICLES Thither, gentle mariner.
Alter thy course for Tyre. When canst thou reach it?   80
SECOND SAILOR By break of day if the wind cease.

85. **Go thy ways:** i.e., go ahead
86. **presently:** immediately (Pericles presumably carries Thaisa's body as he exits.)

3.2 The body of Thaisa washes ashore in Ephesus, where she is revived by a physician named Lord Cerimon.

___

3. **meat:** food
8. **ministered to nature:** i.e., applied or administered to a person's physical constitution
9. **recover:** cure
10. **'pothecary:** apothecary, druggist
16. **bleak:** i.e., exposed
17. **as:** i.e., **as** if

Lucina. (1.1.9; 3.1.10)
From Vincenzo Cartari, *Le imagini de gli dei de gli antichi . . .* (1609).

PERICLES   O, make for Tarsus!
  There will I visit Cleon, for the babe
  Cannot hold out to Tyrus. There I'll leave it
  At careful nursing. Go thy ways, good mariner.   85
  I'll bring the body presently.
                               ⌜*They*⌝ *exit.*

⌜Scene 2⌝

Enter Lord Cerimon with ⌜*two Suppliants.*⌝

CERIMON   Philemon, ho!

Enter Philemon.

PHILEMON   Doth my lord call?
CERIMON   Get fire and meat for these poor men.
  'T has been a turbulent and stormy night.
                              ⌜*Philemon exits.*⌝
⌜FIRST SUPPLIANT⌝
  I have been in many; but such a night as this,   5
  Till now, I ne'er endured.
CERIMON
  Your master will be dead ere you return.
  There's nothing can be ministered to nature
  That can recover him. ⌜*To Second Suppliant.*⌝ Give
    this to the 'pothecary,   10
  And tell me how it works.   ⌜*Suppliants exit.*⌝

Enter two Gentlemen.

FIRST GENTLEMAN   Good morrow.
SECOND GENTLEMAN   Good morrow to your Lordship.
CERIMON
  Gentlemen, why do you stir so early?
FIRST GENTLEMAN   Sir,   15
  Our lodgings, standing bleak upon the sea,
  Shook as the earth did quake.

18. **principals:** main posts, rafters, or braces of a building

22. **husbandry:** i.e., virtue as household managers

25. **Rich tire:** luxurious accoutrements (such as bed hangings or pillows that would lead to **golden slumber** (line 26)

28. **conversant:** occupied, concerned; **pain:** pains, trouble, effort

30–31. **I . . . were:** i.e., **I** have always believed that **virtue** and skill **were**

33. **darken and expend:** i.e., put (**nobleness**) under a shadow and consume (**riches**) in spending

36. **physic:** medicine

36–40. **secret art . . . stones:** See longer note, page 194. **secret:** known only to a select few **art:** learning, skill **turning o'er authorities:** i.e., reading the pages of authoritative texts **to my aid:** perhaps, (brought) **to my** assistance **vegetives:** plants, herbs

44. **more:** greater

45. **tottering honor:** wavering or vacillating fame or reputation (the **nobleness** of line 32)

46. **bags:** moneybags, purses (the **riches** of line 32)

47. **To please the fool and death:** See longer note, page 195, and picture, page 150.

48. **Ephesus:** This ancient Greek city was famous as the site of "the Temple of Diana," one of the seven wonders of the world. (This "temple of the Great Goddess Diana" features prominently in Acts 19.) See map, page xii.

50. **creatures:** creations (Cerimon, having **restored** them through his medicine, has, in effect, created them.)

The very principals did seem to rend
And all to topple. Pure surprise and fear
Made me to quit the house.   20

SECOND GENTLEMAN
That is the cause we trouble you so early.
'Tis not our husbandry.

CERIMON   O, you say well.

FIRST GENTLEMAN
But I much marvel that your Lordship, having
Rich tire about you, should at these early hours   25
Shake off the golden slumber of repose.
'Tis most strange
Nature should be so conversant with pain,
Being thereto not compelled.

CERIMON   I hold it ever   30
Virtue and cunning were endowments greater
Than nobleness and riches. Careless heirs
May the two latter darken and expend,
But immortality attends the former,
Making a man a god. 'Tis known I ever   35
Have studied physic, through which secret art,
By turning o'er authorities, I have,
Together with my practice, made familiar
To me and to my aid the blessed infusions
That dwells in vegetives, in metals, stones;   40
And can speak of the disturbances
That Nature works, and of her cures; which doth
   give me
A more content in course of true delight
Than to be thirsty after tottering honor,   45
Or tie my pleasure up in silken bags
To please the fool and death.

SECOND GENTLEMAN
Your Honor has through Ephesus poured forth
Your charity, and hundreds call themselves
Your creatures, who by you have been restored;   50

51. **not:** i.e., not only; **pain:** i.e., pains, efforts

52. **still:** always, constantly

58. **wrack:** shipwreck

62. **straight:** straightway, at once

63. **o'ercharged with gold:** i.e., distressed by being too full of **gold**

64. **'Tis . . . us:** perhaps, it is (by) Fortune's **good** exercise of force (that) the sea **belches** this (chest full of **gold**) on our shores (See note to **Fortune,** 2 Chor. 37.)

71. **Soft:** i.e., wait a minute; **sense:** i.e., olfactory **sense**

74. **corse:** corpse

76. **Shrouded in cloth of state:** wrapped in rich fabric used by royalty (with wordplay on **shrouded** as "prepared for burial," as in picture below); **balmed:** made fragrant; **entreasured:** stored as if a treasure

77. **passport:** i.e., a letter as if authorizing the corpse's journey

A corpse in a shroud.
From [Richard Day,] *A booke of christian prayers* . . . (1578).

And not your knowledge, your personal pain, but even
Your purse, still open, hath built Lord Cerimon
Such strong renown, as time shall never—

Enter two or three ⌐Servants¬ with a chest.

SERVANT
So, lift there.
CERIMON   What's that?   55
SERVANT   Sir, even now
Did the sea toss up upon our shore this chest.
'Tis of some wrack.
CERIMON   Set 't down. Let's look upon 't.
SECOND GENTLEMAN
'Tis like a coffin, sir.   60
CERIMON   What e'er it be,
'Tis wondrous heavy. Wrench it open straight.
If the sea's stomach be o'ercharged with gold,
'Tis a good constraint of Fortune it belches upon us.
SECOND GENTLEMAN
'Tis so, my lord.   65
CERIMON   How close 'tis caulked and ⌐bitumed!¬
Did the sea cast it up?
SERVANT
I never saw so huge a billow, sir,
As tossed it upon shore.
CERIMON   Wrench it open.   70
Soft! It smells most sweetly in my sense.
SECOND GENTLEMAN   A delicate odor.
CERIMON
As ever hit my nostril. So, up with it.
                            ⌐*They open the chest.*¬
O, you most potent gods! What's here? A corse?
SECOND GENTLEMAN   Most strange!   75
CERIMON
Shrouded in cloth of state, balmed and entreasured
With full bags of spices. A passport too!

78. **Apollo:** Roman god of medicine and of learning; **perfect me in the characters:** i.e., instruct me so that I can read the writing (either the language or the handwriting)

82. **mundane:** earthly; **cost:** i.e., treasure (literally, costly object)

83. **Who:** i.e., whoever

85. **for a fee:** i.e., as a reward

88. **chanced:** occurred; **tonight:** i.e., last night

91. **rough:** harsh

93. **closet:** private room

94. **usurp on:** assume authority over

96. **o'erpressed:** oppressed

98. **appliance:** i.e., medicine (literally, a thing applied as means to an end)

99. **Well said:** i.e., **well** done

100. **rough:** discordant

101. **beseech:** i.e., I implore

102. **viol:** See longer note, page 195.

103. **How thou stirr'st:** a sarcastic reprimand accusing a servant or a musician of moving too slowly; **block:** blockhead

106. **entranced:** thrown into a trance

Apollo, perfect me in the characters.
⌜*He reads.*⌝

> Here I give to understand,
> If e'er this coffin drives aland,　　　　　　　　　80
> I, King Pericles, have lost
> This queen, worth all our mundane cost.
> Who finds her, give her burying.
> She was the daughter of a king.
> Besides this treasure for a fee,　　　　　　　　　85
> The gods requite his charity.

If thou livest, Pericles, thou hast a heart
That ever cracks for woe. This chanced tonight.

SECOND GENTLEMAN
Most likely, sir.

CERIMON　　　　　　　Nay, certainly tonight,　　　90
For look how fresh she looks. They were too rough
That threw her in the sea.—Make a fire within;
Fetch hither all my boxes in my closet.
　　　　　　　　　　　　　　⌜*A servant exits.*⌝

Death may usurp on nature many hours,
And yet the fire of life kindle again　　　　　　　95
The o'erpressed spirits. I heard of an Egyptian
That had nine hours lain dead,
Who was by good appliance recoverèd.

　　　Enter one with ⌜*boxes,*⌝ *napkins, and fire.*

Well said, well said! The fire and cloths.
The rough and woeful music that we have,　　　　100
Cause it to sound, beseech you. ⌜*Music sounds.*⌝ The
　viol once more!
How thou stirr'st, thou block! The music there.
　　　　　　　　　　　　　　⌜*Music sounds.*⌝

I pray you, give her air. Gentlemen,
This queen will live. Nature awakes a ⌜warm⌝ breath　105
Out of her. She hath not been entranced

107. **gins to blow:** begins to blossom
116. **water:** transparency and luster
120. **Diana:** goddess of chastity and of the moon (See pictures, pages 76 and 178.)
124. **gentle:** a complimentary epithet
127. **is mortal:** i.e., would be fatal
128. **Aesculapius:** the god of healing in classical mythology (See picture below.)

3.3 Pericles leaves the infant, Marina, in the care of Cleon and Dionyza and sails for Tyre.

―――――――

3. **litigious:** contentious
4. **Take:** receive
5. **Make up:** supply; **rest:** remainder (that I owe you); **upon:** i.e., to

Aesculapius. (3.2.128)
From Giovanni Battista Cavalleriis, *Antiquarum statuarum . . .* (1585–94).

Above five hours. See how she gins to blow
Into life's flower again.

FIRST GENTLEMAN   The heavens, through you,
Increase our wonder, and sets up your fame   110
Forever.

CERIMON   She is alive. Behold her eyelids—
Cases to those heavenly jewels which Pericles hath
    lost—
Begin to part their fringes of bright gold.   115
The diamonds of a most praised water doth
Appear to make the world twice rich.—Live,
And make us weep to hear your fate, fair creature,
Rare as you seem to be.

                           She moves.

THAISA   O dear Diana,   120
Where am I? Where's my lord? What world is this?

SECOND GENTLEMAN   Is not this strange?

FIRST GENTLEMAN   Most rare!

CERIMON   Hush, my gentle neighbors!
Lend me your hands. To the next chamber bear her.   125
Get linen. Now this matter must be looked to,
For her relapse is mortal. Come, come;
And Aesculapius guide us.

          They carry her away ⌜as⌝ they all exit.

⌜Scene 3⌝

Enter Pericles, at Tarsus, with Cleon and Dionyza, ⌜and
Lychorida with the child.⌝

PERICLES
Most honored Cleon, I must needs be gone.
My twelve months are expired, and Tyrus stands
In a litigious peace. You and your lady
Take from my heart all thankfulness. The gods
Make up the rest upon you.   5

6. **Your shakes of:** i.e., the damaging blows given you by

8. **glance:** i.e., deal glancing blows; **full wond'ringly:** perhaps, causing much amazement; or, perhaps, affecting us strangely

9. **Fates:** See note to 1.2.116. **pleased:** i.e., willed (that)

16. **for:** since; **born at sea:** The word *marine* comes from the Latin *mare,* the **sea.**

17. **withal:** with

20. **mannered . . . born:** i.e., well-**mannered,** just **as she is** well-**born**

22. **corn:** grain, wheat

24. **thought on:** remembered; **neglection:** neglect

31. **to 't:** i.e., to do so

33. **Diana:** See note to 3.2.120.

35. **show ill:** appear **ill**-mannered or unattractive

36. **blessèd in your care:** i.e., fortunate in the **care** you provide

A storm at sea.
From Lodovico Dolce, *Imprese nobili* . . . (1583).

CLEON
  Your shakes of fortune, though they haunt you
    mortally,
  Yet glance full wond'ringly on us.

DIONYZA
  O, your sweet queen! That the strict Fates had pleased
  You had brought her hither to have blessed mine   10
    eyes with her!

PERICLES
  We cannot but obey the powers above us.
  Could I rage and roar as doth the sea
  She lies in, yet the end must be as 'tis.
  My gentle babe Marina,   15
  Whom, for she was born at sea, I have named so,
  Here I charge your charity withal,
  Leaving her the infant of your care,
  Beseeching you to give her princely training,
  That she may be mannered as she is born.   20

CLEON   Fear not, my lord, but think
  Your Grace, that fed my country with your corn,
  For which the people's prayers still fall upon you,
  Must in your child be thought on. If neglection
  Should therein make me vile, the common body,   25
  By you relieved, would force me to my duty.
  But if to that my nature need a spur,
  The gods revenge it upon me and mine,
  To the end of generation!

PERICLES   I believe you.   30
  Your honor and your goodness teach me to 't
  Without your vows.—Till she be married, madam,
  By bright Diana, whom we honor, all
  ⌜Unscissored⌝ shall this hair of mine remain,
  Though I show ⌜ill⌝ in 't. So I take my leave.   35
  Good madam, make me blessèd in your care
  In bringing up my child.

39. **respect:** regard, consideration

43. **maskèd Neptune:** i.e., (1) sea which is masking its dangers; or (2) always deceptive sea; or (3) sea wearing a different face from what it showed you before

47. **grace:** favor

3.4 In Ephesus, Thaisa decides to become a votaress at the temple of Diana.

2. **coffer:** chest, coffin

3. **character:** handwriting

4. **shipped:** embarked

5. **on my bearing time:** i.e., as labor began (Many editions use "eaning **time,**" but *eaning* was used only for the delivery of lambs. Another editorial choice is "groaning **time.**")

8. **I . . . again:** In Gower, she believes that her husband has drowned.

9. **vestal . . . to:** i.e., **take** on a life of chastity (literally, put on the clothing of a **vestal** virgin) See longer note, page 196, and picture, page 110.

12. **purpose:** are resolved to perform; **Diana's temple:** See note to 3.2.48.

DIONYZA   I have one myself,
  Who shall not be more dear to my respect
  Than yours, my lord.   40

PERICLES   Madam, my thanks and prayers.

CLEON
  We'll bring your Grace e'en to the edge o' th' shore,
  Then give you up to the maskèd Neptune
  And the gentlest winds of heaven.

PERICLES
  I will embrace your offer.—Come, dearest madam.— 45
  O, no tears, Lychorida, no tears!
  Look to your little mistress, on whose grace
  You may depend hereafter.—Come, my lord.
                                ⌜*They exit.*⌝

⌜Scene 4⌝

Enter Cerimon and Thaisa.

CERIMON
  Madam, this letter and some certain jewels
  Lay with you in your coffer, which are
  At your command. Know you the character?
                      ⌜*He shows her the letter.*⌝

THAISA
  It is my lord's. That I was shipped at sea
  I well remember, even on my ⌜bearing⌝ time,   5
  But whether there delivered, by the holy gods
  I cannot rightly say. But since King Pericles,
  My wedded lord, I ne'er shall see again,
  A vestal livery will I take me to,
  And never more have joy.   10

CERIMON   Madam, if this
  You purpose as you speak, Diana's temple
  Is not distant far, where you may abide

14. **date:** term of life

A vestal virgin. (3.4.9; 4.5.7)
From Johann Basilius Herold, *Heydenweldt* . . . [1554].

Till your date expire. Moreover, if you
Please, a niece of mine shall there attend you.   15

THAISA
  My recompense is thanks, that's all;
  Yet my good will is great, though the gift small.
                                ⌜*They*⌝ *exit.*

PERICLES,

Prince of Tyre

ACT 4

4 Chorus Gower carries the story forward fourteen years, focusing on the young Marina. Her beauty and talents arouse murderous hatred in Dionyza, whose own daughter cannot compare with Marina.

---

4. **there 's:** i.e., there she is; **votaress:** woman bound by vows to a religious life

6. **scene:** play, performance

8. **letters:** literature

10–11. **both . . . wonder:** perhaps, **both** her artistry and the **wonder** it creates

12. **wrack:** destruction, ruin

14. **take off:** destroy, cut **off; treason's:** treachery's

15. **in this kind:** Editors have suggested that this means "in the same category as Marina."

18. **Hight:** was called

21. **sleided silk:** a variant of (1) sleaved **silk** (i.e., **silk** divided into filaments) or (2) sleave **silk** (i.e., coarse silk capable of being divided)

22. **small:** slender

An hourglass. (5.2.1)
From August Casimir Redel, *Apophtegmata symbolica* . . . [n.d.].

⌜ACT 4⌝

Enter Gower.

⌜GOWER⌝
Imagine Pericles arrived at Tyre,
Welcomed and settled to his own desire.
His woeful queen we leave at Ephesus,
Unto Diana there 's a votaress.
Now to Marina bend your mind,   5
Whom our fast-growing scene must find
At Tarsus, and by Cleon trained
In ⌜music,⌝ letters; who hath gained
Of education all the grace
Which makes high both the art and place   10
Of general wonder. But, alack,
That monster envy, oft the wrack
Of earnèd praise, Marina's life
⌜Seeks⌝ to take off by treason's knife.
And in this kind our Cleon hath   15
One daughter and a full grown wench,
Even ⌜ripe⌝ for marriage ⌜rite.⌝ This maid
Hight Philoten, and it is said
For certain in our story she
Would ever with Marina be.   20
Be 't when they weaved the sleided silk
With fingers long, small, white as milk;
Or when she would with sharp needle wound
The cambric, which she made more sound

115

26. **the night bird:** here, the nightingale

27. **still:** constantly; **records with moan:** i.e., (1) sings sadly; (2) recalls with sadness (The nightingale, according to mythology, was once a princess who was raped and whose tongue was cut out.)

28. **with rich and constant pen:** i.e., with writings both elaborate and devoted

29. **Vail:** do homage; **Dian:** Diana; **still:** always

31. **absolute:** free from imperfection

32–33. **With . . . white:** i.e., so might the crow compete **with** one of Venus's doves in the whiteness of its **feathers** (Doves were sacred to Venus, one of whose homes was in **Paphos,** a city on the island of Cyprus.) See map, page xii.

34. **debts:** obligations

35. **given:** bestowed as a gift; **darks:** obscures

37. **envy rare:** exceptional malice

41. **stead:** aid, assist

44. **pregnant:** receptive, ready

45. **Prest:** i.e., impressed, forced to serve; or, perhaps, prepared; **event:** outcome

46. **commend to your content:** i.e., present for your pleasure

47–49. **I carry . . . convey:** Wordplay on **lame** (as "crippled" and "metrically defective"), on **feet** (as divisions of a verse), and on **convey** (as "transport" and "communicate") allows Gower to present the notion of his verse carrying the proverbial **wingèd Time.** (See picture, page 122.)   **Post:** in haste

4.1 Dionyza's hired murderer, Leonine, is prevented from murdering Marina by pirates, who carry her away to their ship.

By hurting it; or when to the lute 25
She sung, and made the night ⌜bird⌝ mute,
That still records with moan; or when
She would with rich and constant pen
Vail to her mistress Dian, still
This Philoten contends in skill 30
With absolute Marina. So
⌜With⌝ the dove of Paphos might the crow
Vie feathers white. Marina gets
All praises, which are paid as debts
And not as given. This so darks 35
In Philoten all graceful marks
That Cleon's wife, with envy rare,
A present murderer does prepare
For good Marina, that her daughter
Might stand peerless by this slaughter. 40
The sooner her vile thoughts to stead,
Lychorida, our nurse, is dead,
And cursèd Dionyza hath
The pregnant instrument of wrath
Prest for this blow. The unborn event 45
I do commend to your content.
Only I ⌜carry⌝ wingèd Time
Post on the lame feet of my rhyme,
Which never could I so convey
Unless your thoughts went on my way. 50
Dionyza does appear,
With Leonine, a murderer.

He exits.

⌜Scene 1⌝

Enter Dionyza with Leonine.

DIONYZA
　Thy oath remember. Thou hast sworn to do 't.
　'Tis but a blow which never shall be known.

3–4. **so soon / To yield:** i.e., (that will) more readily or easily **yield**

4–6. **Let . . . nicely:** These lines present a major problem to editors. Their general sense seems to be, "Don't **let conscience** deter you (from killing Marina) by awaking compassion in your **bosom**." **nicely:** perhaps, scrupulously; or, perhaps, fastidiously

13. **her only mistress':** Since Marina is **weeping for** Lychorida's **death,** many editions change **mistress'** to "nurse's."

15. **Tellus:** i.e., the earth (**Tellus** was goddess of the earth. See picture, page 144.) **weed:** apparel, clothing

16. **thy green:** perhaps, the grassy plot over Lychorida's grave

25. **consume . . . sorrowing:** It was believed that sighs of sorrow consumed the heart's **blood.** (See *Romeo and Juliet:* "Dry sorrow drinks our **blood**" [3.5.59].)

26. **Have . . . me:** i.e., Let **me** be your **nurse. favor 's:** appearance has, face has

28. **O'er the sea marge:** i.e., along the shore of the sea

29. **quick:** i.e., brisk

30. **stomach:** appetite

34. **bereave:** deprive

Thou canst not do a thing in the world so soon
To yield thee so much profit. Let not conscience,
Which is but cold in flaming, thy bosom inflame   5
Too nicely. Nor let pity, which even women
Have cast off, melt thee; but be a soldier
To thy purpose.

LEONINE   I will do 't; but yet
She is a goodly creature.   10

DIONYZA   The fitter, then,
The gods should have her. Here she comes weeping
For her only mistress' death. Thou art resolved?

LEONINE   I am resolved.

Enter Marina with a basket of flowers.

MARINA
No, I will rob Tellus of her weed   15
To strew thy green with flowers. The yellows, blues,
The purple violets and marigolds
Shall as a carpet hang upon thy grave
While summer days doth last. Ay me, poor maid,
Born in a tempest when my mother died,   20
This world to me is ⌈as⌉ a lasting storm,
Whirring me from my friends.

DIONYZA
How now, Marina? Why do you keep alone?
How chance my daughter is not with you?
Do not consume your blood with sorrowing.   25
Have you a nurse of me! Lord, how your favor 's
Changed with this unprofitable woe.
Come, give me your flowers. ⌈O'er the sea marge⌉
Walk with Leonine. The air is quick there,
And it pierces and sharpens the stomach.—Come,   30
   Leonine,
Take her by the arm. Walk with her.

MARINA   No,
I pray you, I'll not bereave you of your servant.

37. **foreign heart:** i.e., a **heart** not of your household or family

39. **paragon to all reports:** i.e., universally acknowledged pattern of excellence; **blasted:** blighted

42. **courses:** proceedings

43. **Reserve:** preserve

45. **Care not for:** i.e., do not concern yourself about

53. **warrant:** assure

55. **softly:** slowly, in a leisurely manner

56. **What:** i.e., well

64. **haling:** pulling

The four winds. (4.1.58–60)
From Giulio Cesare Capaccio, *Delle imprese trattato* . . . (1592).

DIONYZA   Come, come.   35
   I love the king your father and yourself
   With more than foreign heart. We every day
   Expect him here. When he shall come and find
   Our paragon to all reports thus blasted,
   He will repent the breadth of his great voyage,   40
   Blame both my lord and me that we have taken
   No care to your best courses. Go, I pray you,
   Walk, and be cheerful once again. Reserve
   That excellent complexion, which did steal
   The eyes of young and old. Care not for me.   45
   I can go home alone.

MARINA   Well, I will go,
   But yet I have no desire to it.

DIONYZA   Come, come,
   I know 'tis good for you.—Walk half an hour,   50
   Leonine, at the least. Remember
   What I have said.

LEONINE   I warrant you, madam.

DIONYZA
   I'll leave you, my sweet lady, for a while.
   Pray walk softly; do not heat your blood.   55
   What, I must have care of you.

MARINA   My thanks, sweet madam.   ⌜*Dionyza exits.*⌝
   Is this wind westerly that blows?

LEONINE   Southwest.

MARINA
   When I was born, the wind was north.   60

LEONINE   Was 't so?

MARINA
   My father, as nurse says, did never fear,
   But cried "Good seamen!" to the sailors,
   Galling his kingly hands haling ropes,
   And, clasping to the mast, endured a sea   65
   That almost burst the deck.

LEONINE   When was this?

70. **ladder-tackle:** i.e., rigging

71. **canvas-climber:** sailor; **Wolt:** i.e., do you want (an obsolete form of "wilt"—i.e., will you); **out:** If the question is addressed to the storm, **out** may refer to the wind's blowing away from the shore; if it is addressed, cruelly, to the sailor, it may refer to his being swept overboard.

72. **dropping industry:** i.e., dripping-wet effort

77. **space:** time

84. **as:** i.e., as far as; **by my troth:** This mild oath, like **la** (line 87) and **Good sooth** (line 99), characterizes Marina as markedly innocent and ladylike.

86. **ill turn:** injury

94. **reason of:** talk about

96. **foreshow:** show forth

98. **caught hurt:** received an injury

"Wingèd Time." (4 Chor. 47; 5.2.15)
From August Casimir Redel, *Apophtegmata symbolica* . . . [n.d.].

MARINA When I was born.
  Never was waves nor wind more violent,
  And from the ladder-tackle washes off   70
  A canvas-climber. "Ha!" says one, "Wolt out?"
  And with a dropping industry they skip
  From stern to stern. The Boatswain whistles, and
  The Master calls and trebles their confusion.

LEONINE Come, say your prayers.   75
            ⌜*He draws his sword.*⌝

MARINA What mean you?

LEONINE
  If you require a little space for prayer,
  I grant it. Pray, but be not tedious, for
  The gods are quick of ear, and I am sworn
  To do my work with haste.   80

MARINA Why will you kill me?

LEONINE To satisfy my lady.

MARINA Why would she have me killed?
  Now, as I can remember, by my troth,
  I never did her hurt in all my life.   85
  I never spake bad word, nor did ill turn
  To any living creature. Believe me, la,
  I never killed a mouse, nor hurt a fly.
  I trod upon a worm against my will,
  But I wept for 't. How have I offended   90
  Wherein my death might yield her any profit
  Or my life imply her any danger?

LEONINE My commission
  Is not to reason of the deed, but do 't.

MARINA
  You will not do 't for all the world, I hope.   95
  You are well-favored, and your looks foreshow
  You have a gentle heart. I saw you lately
  When you caught hurt in parting two that fought.
  Good sooth, it showed well in you. Do so now.

104. **Hold:** stop

106. **Half-part:** This generally means "half," but here it may mean "share and share alike."

107. **suddenly:** at once

107 SD. **Enter Leonine:** It is possible that **Leonine,** instead of running offstage at line 104, remains cowering onstage. He would, in that case, here come forward.

108. **roguing:** i.e., vagrant, roving (Rogues were idle vagrants.)

111. **see further:** i.e., look around

112. **please themselves upon:** i.e., rape

114. **Whom:** i.e., she **whom**

4.2 Marina is sold by the pirates to a brothel in Mytilene.

_____

3. **narrowly:** carefully, closely; **Mytilene:** a port city on the island of Lesbos in the Aegean Sea (See map, page xii.)

4. **gallants:** pleasure-seeking men; **this mart:** i.e., the most recent **mart,** a periodic gathering of buyers and sellers

5. **wenchless:** i.e., unprovided with prostitutes

6. **creatures:** i.e., whores

7. **but poor three:** i.e., only **three**

Your lady seeks my life. Come you between,   100
And save poor me, the weaker.

LEONINE   I am sworn
And will dispatch.   ⌜*He seizes her.*⌝

                Enter Pirates.

FIRST PIRATE   Hold, villain!   ⌜*Leonine runs offstage.*⌝
SECOND PIRATE   A prize, a prize!   ⌜*He seizes Marina.*⌝ 105
THIRD PIRATE   Half-part, mates, half-part. Come, let's
    have her aboard suddenly.
                          ⌜*They*⌝ exit, ⌜*carrying Marina.*⌝

                Enter Leonine.

LEONINE
These roguing thieves serve the great pirate Valdes,
And they have seized Marina. Let her go.
There's no hope she will return. I'll swear she's dead, 110
And thrown into the sea. But I'll see further.
Perhaps they will but please themselves upon her,
Not carry her aboard. If she remain,
Whom they have ravished must by me be slain.
                                    He exits.

                ⌜*Scene 2*⌝

          Enter ⌜*Pander, Bawd, and Bolt.*⌝

PANDER   Bolt!
BOLT   Sir?
PANDER   Search the market narrowly. Mytilene is full
    of gallants. We lost too much money this mart by
    being too wenchless.   5
BAWD   We were never so much out of creatures. We
    have but poor three, and they can do no more than
    they can do; and they with continual action are
    even as good as rotten.

11–12. If . . . trade: i.e., if we don't use our **conscience** in our profession

13–14. 'Tis . . . bastards: The Bawd may be claiming (1) that she has helped their **trade prosper** by raising bastard children; or (2) that her caring for such children demonstrates the **conscience** (line 11) of their **trade.**

16. to eleven: i.e., **to** the age of **eleven; brought . . . again:** i.e., put them into service at the brothel

20. sodden: i.e., water-logged (from soaking in the sweating tubs used for treating venereal disease) See picture, page 148.

21–22. a' conscience: i.e., truly

22. Transylvanian: man from Transylvania

23. baggage: strumpet, whore

24. pooped: infected (with venereal disease) The word *poop* was used as a vulgar term for the female genitals.

25. roast-meat: i.e., a feast

27. chequins: gold coins

27–28. were . . . proportion: i.e., would be a nice portion

28. give over: cease working, retire

29. get: make money

31. credit: good name

31–32. commodity: profit, gain

32. wages not with: i.e., does not rival

33. in our youths: i.e., now (perhaps said ironically)

34. estate: fortune, property

(continued)

PANDER Therefore let's have fresh ones, whate'er we 10
pay for them. If there be not a conscience to be
used in every trade, we shall never prosper.

BAWD Thou sayst true. 'Tis not our bringing up of poor
bastards—as I think I have brought up some
eleven— 15

BOLT Ay, to eleven, and brought them down again. But
shall I search the market?

BAWD What else, man? The stuff we have, a strong
wind will blow it to pieces, they are so pitifully
sodden. 20

PANDER Thou sayst true. There's two unwholesome, a'
conscience. The poor Transylvanian is dead that
lay with the little baggage.

BOLT Ay, she quickly pooped him. She made him
roast-meat for worms. But I'll go search the mar- 25
ket.   *He exits.*

PANDER Three or four thousand chequins were as
pretty a proportion to live quietly, and so give over.

BAWD Why to give over, I pray you? Is it a shame to get
when we are old? 30

PANDER O, our credit comes not in like the commodity, nor the commodity wages not with the danger.
Therefore, if in our youths we could pick up some
pretty estate, 'twere not amiss to keep our door
hatched. Besides, the sore terms we stand upon 35
with the gods will be strong with us for giving o'er.

BAWD Come, other sorts offend as well as we.

PANDER As well as we? Ay, and better too; we offend
worse. Neither is our profession any trade; it's no
calling. But here comes Bolt. 40

Enter Bolt with the Pirates and Marina.

BOLT Come your ways, my masters. You say she's a
virgin?

⌜PIRATE⌝ O, sir, we doubt it not.

35. **hatched:** closed; **the sore . . . upon:** i.e., our grievous standing

36. **strong with us:** i.e., a powerful incentive

37. **sorts:** i.e., professions; **as well as:** in addition to (Line 38 uses the phrase to mean "in as virtuous a way as.")

39. **trade:** perhaps, lawful **trade**

40. **calling:** This name for one's occupation, like *vocation*, carries religious overtones.

41. **Come your ways:** i.e., **come** along

44. **gone through:** perhaps, completed (the negotiations for); **piece:** woman

46. **earnest:** earnest money, down payment

47. **qualities:** natural gifts, accomplishments

49. **necessity of:** i.e., requisite

50. **can:** i.e., (the lack of which) **can**

52. **be bated . . . pieces:** i.e., get the price reduced **one doit** below **a thousand** (gold) **pieces   bated:** reduced   **doit:** an almost worthless small Dutch coin

54. **presently:** immediately

55. **raw:** untrained

56. **entertainment:** treatment (of customers)

57. **take you . . . her:** i.e., write down (or, ascertain, or, carry with you) her distinctive features

58. **warrant:** guarantee

73. **are light:** i.e., have arrived, have fallen

73–74. **like to live:** likely to survive; or, likely to remain

BOLT   Master, I have gone through for this piece you
see. If you like her, so; if not, I have lost my   45
earnest.

BAWD   Bolt, has she any qualities?

BOLT   She has a good face, speaks well, and has excellent good clothes. There's no farther necessity of
qualities can make her be refused.   50

BAWD   What's her price, Bolt?

BOLT   I cannot be bated one doit of a thousand pieces.

PANDER   Well, follow me, my masters; you shall have
your money presently.—Wife, take her in. Instruct
her what she has to do, that she may not be raw in   55
her entertainment.   ⌜*He exits with Pirates.*⌝

BAWD   Bolt, take you the marks of her: the color of her
hair, complexion, height, her age, with warrant of
her virginity, and cry "He that will give most shall
have her first." Such a maidenhead were no cheap   60
thing, if men were as they have been. Get this done
as I command you.

BOLT   Performance shall follow.   *He exits.*

MARINA
Alack that Leonine was so slack, so slow!
He should have struck, not spoke. Or that these   65
pirates,
Not enough barbarous, had ⌜but⌝ o'erboard thrown me
For to seek my mother.

BAWD   Why lament you, pretty one?

MARINA   That I am pretty.   70

BAWD   Come, the gods have done their part in you.

MARINA   I accuse them not.

BAWD   You are light into my hands, where you are like
to live.

MARINA   The more my fault, to 'scape his hands where   75
I was to die.

BAWD   Ay, and you shall live in pleasure.

MARINA   No.

81. **difference:** perhaps, variety; **of all complexions:** i.e., of (men of) every sort; **What:** an exclamation introducing a question

84. **an:** if

86. **honest:** chaste (the standard meaning when applied to women)

87. **Marry:** a mild oath; **whip the gosling:** confound the young goose

95. **cried her:** i.e., advertised her attractions, announced her availability

103. **an:** i.e., as if

108. **cowers i' the hams:** i.e., has bent knees and back (presumably from syphilis)

109. **Monsieur Verolles:** i.e., Mr. Pox (In French, *la verole* means "pox," a name for venereal disease.)

110. **offered:** attempted

BAWD Yes, indeed shall you, and taste gentlemen of all
  fashions. You shall fare well; you shall have the   80
  difference of all complexions. What, do you stop
  your ears?
MARINA Are you a woman?
BAWD What would you have me be, an I be not a
  woman?   85
MARINA An honest woman, or not a woman.
BAWD Marry, whip the gosling! I think I shall have
  something to do with you. Come, you're a young
  foolish sapling, and must be bowed as I would
  have you.   90
MARINA The gods defend me!
BAWD If it please the gods to defend you by men, then
  men must comfort you, men must feed you, men
  stir you up. Bolt's returned.

⌜*Enter Bolt.*⌝

  Now, sir, hast thou cried her through the market?   95
BOLT I have cried her almost to the number of her
  hairs. I have drawn her picture with my voice.
BAWD And I prithee tell me, how dost thou find the in-
  clination of the people, especially of the younger
  sort?   100
BOLT Faith, they listened to me as they would have
  hearkened to their father's testament. There was a
  Spaniard's mouth watered an he went to bed to her
  very description.
BAWD We shall have him here tomorrow with his best   105
  ruff on.
BOLT Tonight, tonight! But, mistress, do you know the
  French knight that cowers i' the hams?
BAWD Who? Monsieur Verolles?
BOLT Ay, he. He offered to cut a caper at the proclama-   110
  tion, but he made a groan at it and swore he would
  see her tomorrow.

113. **his disease:** Syphilis was called "the French **disease.**"

114. **repair:** renew

115–16. **in our . . . sun:** i.e., under the **shadow** of **our** roof to spend **his** (French) **crowns**

117. **of every:** i.e., from **every**

118. **lodge them with:** i.e., become their lodging by means of; **this sign:** perhaps indicating (1) Marina, or (2) his list of Marina's "marks"

124. **Seldom but:** i.e., often

125. **mere:** downright

127. **take her home:** i.e., explain it to her (To speak **home** is to speak plainly.)

129. **present:** immediate

130–31. **your bride:** i.e., even a **bride**

131. **that:** i.e., her first sexual experience; **way:** path, course of action

132. **with warrant:** i.e., legally

134. **joint:** large cut of roast meat (here, Marina herself, of whom Bolt is promised **a morsel** [line 135])

141. **sojourner:** guest, lodger

142. **by custom:** i.e., through our getting customers

147. **awake . . . eels:** That "**thunder** looses **beds of eels**" was a common belief, and perhaps a proverb.

BAWD   Well, well, as for him, he brought his disease
   hither; here he does but repair it. I know he will
   come in our shadow, to scatter his crowns in the   115
   sun.
BOLT   Well, if we had of every nation a traveler, we
   should lodge them with this sign.
BAWD, ⌜to Marina⌝ Pray you, come hither awhile. You
   have fortunes coming upon you. Mark me: you   120
   must seem to do that fearfully which you commit
   willingly, despise profit where you have most gain.
   To weep that you live as you do makes pity in your
   lovers. Seldom but that pity begets you a good
   opinion, and that opinion a mere profit.   125
MARINA   I understand you not.
BOLT   O, take her home, mistress, take her home!
   These blushes of hers must be quenched with
   some present practice.
⌜BAWD⌝ Thou sayst true, i' faith, so they must, for your   130
   bride goes to that with shame which is her way to
   go with warrant.
BOLT   Faith, some do and some do not. But, mistress,
   if I have bargained for the joint—
BAWD   Thou mayst cut a morsel off the spit.   135
BOLT   I may so.
BAWD   Who should deny it? Come, young one, I like
   the manner of your garments well.
BOLT   Ay, by my faith, they shall not be changed yet.
BAWD   Bolt, spend thou that in the town. (⌜She gives him   140
   money.⌝) Report what a sojourner we have. You'll
   lose nothing by custom. When Nature framed this
   piece, she meant thee a good turn. Therefore say
   what a paragon she is, and thou hast the harvest
   out of thine own report.   145
BOLT   I warrant you, mistress, thunder shall not so
   awake the beds of eels as my giving out her beauty
   stirs up the lewdly inclined. I'll bring home some
   tonight.

152. **Untied:** Marina presumably means "Tied" rather than **untied.**

153. **Diana:** See note to 3.2.120.

154. **pray you:** i.e., I ask you

4.3 Dionyza, after Leonine has (falsely) reported Marina's death, now justifies her actions to a horrified Cleon.

---

7. **Much . . . virtue:** i.e., even higher **in virtue** than in her noble birth

9. **I' the . . . compare:** i.e., in a just comparison

11. **drunk to him:** i.e., toasted him (from the poisoned cup)

12. **Becoming . . . face:** perhaps, "suiting (the ugliness of) your **face**" (Editors often emend **face** to "fact," which meant "deed.")

14. **Fates:** See note to 1.2.116.

15. **ever:** always, at all times

16. **cross:** contradict

17. **impious:** i.e., disloyal

18. **honest attribute:** i.e., reputation for honesty

BAWD, ⌜*to Marina*⌝ Come your ways. Follow me.   150

MARINA
  If fires be hot, knives sharp, or waters deep,
  Untied I still my virgin knot will keep.
  Diana aid my purpose!

BAWD   What have we to do with Diana, pray you? Will
    you go with us?   155

⌜*They*⌝ *exit.*

⌜Scene 3⌝

Enter Cleon and Dionyza.

DIONYZA
  Why, ⌜are⌝ you foolish? Can it be undone?

CLEON
  O Dionyza, such a piece of slaughter
  The sun and moon ne'er looked upon!

DIONYZA   I think you'll turn a child again.

CLEON
  Were I chief lord of all this spacious world,   5
  I'd give it to undo the deed. ⌜A⌝ lady
  Much less in blood than virtue, yet a princess
  To equal any single crown o' th' earth
  I' the justice of compare. O villain Leonine,
  Whom thou hast poisoned too!   10
  If thou hadst drunk to him, 't had been a kindness
  Becoming well thy face. What canst thou say
  When noble Pericles shall demand his child?

DIONYZA
  That she is dead. Nurses are not the Fates.
  To foster ⌜is⌝ not ever to preserve.   15
  She died at night; I'll say so. Who can cross it
  Unless you play the impious innocent
  And, for an honest attribute, cry out
  "She died by foul play!"

20. **go to:** an exclamation of impatience or anger

24. **wrens:** In folktales and ballads, murders are often revealed by birds.

25. **open:** disclose, reveal

29. **but . . . added:** i.e., merely gave his approval (after the fact)

30. **prime:** i.e., original

31. **courses:** perhaps, lines of succession (i.e., family lines)

35. **distain:** outshine

36. **fortunes:** i.e., success

38. **blurted at:** i.e., treated with contempt; **held a malkin:** considered a slattern

42. **greets:** perhaps, addresses itself to; or, perhaps, gratifies; **kindness:** natural family affection

49. **characters:** letters

52. **Harpy:** a mythological rapacious creature with a bird's wings and talons and a woman's face (See picture below.)

A Harpy. (4.3.52)
From Conrad Lycosthenes, *Prodigiorum* . . . [1557].

CLEON   O, go to. Well, well,   20
　　Of all the faults beneath the heavens, the gods
　　Do like this worst.
DIONYZA   Be one of those that thinks
　　The petty wrens of Tarsus will fly hence
　　And open this to Pericles. I do shame   25
　　To think of what a noble strain you are,
　　And of how coward a spirit.
CLEON   To such proceeding
　　Whoever but his approbation added,
　　Though not his ⌈prime⌉ consent, he did not flow   30
　　From honorable courses.
DIONYZA   Be it so, then.
　　Yet none does know but you how she came dead,
　　Nor none can know, Leonine being gone.
　　She did ⌈distain⌉ my child and stood between   35
　　Her and her fortunes. None would look on her,
　　But cast their gazes on Marina's face,
　　Whilst ours was blurted at and held a malkin
　　Not worth the time of day. It pierced me through,
　　And though you call my course unnatural,   40
　　You not your child well loving, yet I find
　　It greets me as an enterprise of kindness
　　Performed to your sole daughter.
CLEON   Heavens forgive it.
DIONYZA   And as for Pericles,   45
　　What should he say? We wept after her hearse,
　　And yet we mourn. Her monument is
　　Almost finished, and her epitaphs
　　In glitt'ring golden characters express
　　A general praise to her, and care in us   50
　　At whose expense 'tis done.
CLEON   Thou art like the Harpy,
　　Which, to betray, dost with thine angel's face
　　Seize with thine eagle's talons.

56. **swear:** affirm by an oath; **winter kills:** i.e., nature (not a human being) **kills**

4.4 Gower tells of Pericles' arrival in Tarsus, his learning of Marina's death, and his vow of perpetual mourning.

————

1. **waste:** consume (i.e., make disappear, telescope, condense)
2. **cockles:** cockle shells (often associated with supernatural sailing or flying); **have . . . for 't:** i.e., **have** (something) if we merely **wish for** it
3. **Making:** perhaps, preparing or proceeding
6. **several clime:** different region
7. **seems:** i.e., seem
8. **learn of:** i.e., **learn** from; **stand in:** i.e., fill in, or bridge
10. **thwarting:** crossing
14. **it:** i.e., Tyre; **bear in mind:** remember
15. **late:** recently
18. **think . . . thought:** i.e., imagine that **thought** is **his pilot**
19. **his steerage:** i.e., the steering of his ship
20. **first is:** perhaps, has already
21. **Like . . . move:** i.e., **see them** silently **move motes:** specks floating in the sunlight

DIONYZA
  You're like one that superstitiously   55
  Do swear to the gods that winter kills the flies.
  But yet I know you'll do as I advise.
                        ⌈*They exit.*⌉

⌈Scene 4⌉

⌈*Enter Gower.*⌉

GOWER
  Thus time we waste, and long leagues make short,
  Sail seas in cockles, have and wish but for 't,
  Making to take our imagination
  From bourn to bourn, region to region.
  By you being pardoned, we commit no crime   5
  To use one language in each several clime
  Where our scenes seems to live. I do beseech you
  To learn of me, who stand ⌈in the⌉ gaps to teach you
  The stages of our story. Pericles
  Is now again thwarting ⌈the⌉ wayward seas,   10
  Attended on by many a lord and knight,
  To see his daughter, all his life's delight.
  Old Helicanus goes along. Behind
  Is left to govern it, you bear in mind,
  Old Escanes, whom Helicanus late   15
  Advanced in time to great and high estate.
  Well-sailing ships and bounteous winds have brought
  This king to Tarsus—think ⌈his⌉ pilot thought;
  So with his steerage shall your thoughts ⌈go on⌉—
  To fetch his daughter home, who first is gone.   20
  Like motes and shadows see them move awhile;
  Your ears unto your eyes I'll reconcile.

⌈*Dumb Show.*⌉

Enter Pericles at one door, with all his train, Cleon and
Dionyza at the other. Cleon shows Pericles the tomb,

22 SD. **sackcloth:** coarse cloth worn as a sign of lamentation; **passion:** overwhelming emotion; vehement grief

23. **foul show:** wicked pretence or simulation

24. **This borrowed passion:** i.e., Cleon and Dionyza's pretended grief; **stands for:** takes the place of

32. **wit:** know

33. **is:** i.e., that is

40. **Thetis:** i.e., the sea (See longer note, page 196, and picture, page 174.) **some part o' th' earth:** i.e., the body of Thaisa (**earth** because, according to Genesis, this is what humans are made from)

42. **Thetis' birth-child:** i.e., Marina

43. **Wherefore she:** i.e., therefore the sea; **stint:** cease

44. **battery:** bombardment; **shores of flint:** i.e., rocky **shores**

45. **visor:** face-concealing mask; **does become:** i.e., suits

48–49. **bear . . . Fortune:** i.e., allow chance to direct his ship   **Lady Fortune:** See note to 2 Chor. 37.

49. **play:** perform

50. **heavy welladay:** sad lamentation

whereat Pericles makes lamentation, puts on sackcloth,
and in a mighty passion departs. ⌜*Cleon and Dionyza exit.*⌝

See how belief may suffer by foul show!
This borrowed passion stands for true old woe.
And Pericles, in sorrow all devoured,   25
With sighs shot through and biggest tears
   o'ershowered,
Leaves Tarsus and again embarks. He swears
Never to wash his face nor cut his hairs.
He ⌜puts⌝ on sackcloth, and to sea. He bears   30
A tempest which his mortal vessel tears,
And yet he rides it out. Now please you wit
The epitaph is for Marina writ
By wicked Dionyza:

The fairest, sweetest, and best lies here,   35
Who withered in her spring of year.
She was of Tyrus, the King's daughter,
On whom foul death hath made this slaughter.
Marina was she called, and at her birth,
Thetis, being proud, swallowed some part o' th' earth.   40
Therefore the earth, fearing to be o'erflowed,
Hath Thetis' birth-child on the heavens bestowed.
Wherefore she does—and swears she'll never stint—
Make raging battery upon shores of flint.

No visor does become black villainy   45
So well as soft and tender flattery.
Let Pericles believe his daughter's dead,
And bear his courses to be orderèd
By Lady Fortune, while our ⌜scene⌝ must play
His daughter's woe and heavy welladay   50
In her unholy service. Patience, then,
And think you now are all in Mytilene.   *He exits.*

4.5 In Mytilene, Marina preserves her virginity through eloquent pleas to her potential customers. We see the effect on two such customers.

---

4. **divinity:** theology

7. **Shall 's:** i.e., **shall** we; **vestals:** i.e., vestal virgins (See longer note to 3.4.9 [page 196], and picture, page 110.)

4.6 Lysimachus, the governor of Mytilene, arrives at the brothel and is so moved (or shamed) by Marina's eloquence that he gives her money, thus enabling her to buy her way out of the brothel.

---

4. **Priapus:** the Greek and Roman **god** of procreation; **undo:** destroy

6. **fitment:** duty, appropriate service; **do me:** i.e., **do,** perform (**Me** is an old form of the dative, as it is in "has **me**" [line 7], and does not affect the meaning.)

7. **quirks:** evasions, quibbles

10. **cheapen a kiss of:** i.e., offer to pay for **a kiss** from

11. **disfurnish:** i.e., deprive

12. **cavalleria:** i.e., cavaliers

13. **the pox upon:** an exclamation of irritation (**The pox** is a venereal disease, as the Bawd points out in line 15.) **greensickness:** i.e., virginal reluctance (See longer note, page 196.)

14. **on 't:** i.e., of it

⌜Scene 5⌝

Enter two Gentlemen.

FIRST GENTLEMAN　Did you ever hear the like?

SECOND GENTLEMAN　No, nor never shall do in such a
place as this, she being once gone.

FIRST GENTLEMAN　But to have divinity preached there!
Did you ever dream of such a thing?　　　　　　　5

SECOND GENTLEMAN　No, no. Come, I am for no more
bawdy houses. Shall 's go hear the vestals sing?

FIRST GENTLEMAN　I'll do anything now that is virtuous,
but I am out of the road of rutting forever.

　　　　　　　　　　　　　　　⌜*They*⌝ *exit.*

⌜Scene 6⌝

Enter ⌜*Bawd, Pander, and Bolt.*⌝

PANDER　Well, I had rather than twice the worth of her
she had ne'er come here.

BAWD　Fie, fie upon her! She's able to freeze the god
Priapus and undo a whole generation. We must
either get her ravished or be rid of her. When she　　5
should do for clients her fitment and do me the
kindness of our profession, she has me her quirks,
her reasons, her master reasons, her prayers, her
knees, that she would make a puritan of the devil if
he should cheapen a kiss of her.　　　　　　　　　10

BOLT　Faith, I must ravish her, or she'll disfurnish us of
all our cavalleria, and make our swearers priests.

PANDER　Now the pox upon her greensickness for me!

BAWD　Faith, there's no way to be rid on 't but by the
way to the pox.　　　　　　　　　　　　　　　15

Enter Lysimachus.

Here comes the Lord Lysimachus disguised.

17. **lown:** man of low birth (Proverbial: **"lord and lown."**)

17–18. **peevish:** perverse, obstinate

18. **give way:** allow liberty of action

19. **How now:** a greeting; **How a:** i.e., what is the price of **a**

21. **to-bless:** i.e., **bless** entirely (In Middle English, *to* as a prefix is an intensive.)

23. **so:** i.e., be **glad**

24. **resorters:** visitors, frequenters

25. **Wholesome . . . you:** i.e., do **you have** a healthy sinner

26. **withal:** with

38. **That:** i.e., speaking modestly; **bawd:** a term applied at the time to male and female procurers

39. **to be:** i.e., for being (or, who claim **to be**)

42. **fair:** beautiful

47. **leave a word:** i.e., permission to speak

51. **honorable man:** i.e., person of high rank

Tellus. (4.1.15)
From Vincenzo Cartari, *Le imagini de gli dei de gli antichi* . . . (1609).

BOLT We should have both lord and lown, if the peevish baggage would but give way to customers.

LYSIMACHUS, ⌜*removing his disguise*⌝ How now! How a
dozen of virginities?   20

BAWD Now the gods to-bless your Honor!

BOLT I am glad to see your Honor in good health.

LYSIMACHUS You may so. 'Tis the better for you that
your resorters stand upon sound legs. How now?
Wholesome iniquity have you that a man may deal   25
withal and defy the surgeon?

BAWD We have here one, sir, if she would—but there
never came her like in Mytilene.

LYSIMACHUS If she'd do the deeds of darkness, thou
wouldst say?   30

BAWD Your Honor knows what 'tis to say, well enough.

LYSIMACHUS Well, call forth, call forth. ⌜*Pander exits.*⌝

BOLT For flesh and blood, sir, white and red, you shall
see a rose; and she were a rose indeed, if she had
but—   35

LYSIMACHUS What, prithee?

BOLT O, sir, I can be modest.

LYSIMACHUS That ⌜dignifies⌝ the renown of a bawd no
less than it gives a good report to a number to be
chaste.   40

⌜*Enter Pander with Marina.*⌝

BAWD Here comes that which grows to the stalk, never
plucked yet, I can assure you. Is she not a fair creature?

LYSIMACHUS Faith, she would serve after a long voyage
at sea. Well, there's for you. ⌜*He gives money.*⌝   45
Leave us.

BAWD I beseech your Honor, give me leave a word, and
I'll have done presently.

LYSIMACHUS I beseech you, do.   ⌜*He moves aside.*⌝

BAWD, ⌜*to Marina*⌝ First, I would have you note this is   50
an honorable man.

52. **so:** i.e., **honorable** (decent, virtuous)

55. **bound:** indebted (used by Marina [line 56] to mean "subject, obligated by duty")

65. **paced:** trained, broken

66. **work her to your manage:** i.e., bring her under your control, make her submit to your handling (**Paced** and **manage** refer to the schooling of horses.)

67. **Go thy ways:** i.e., **go,** depart

71. **but I shall offend:** i.e., without giving offense

77. **gamester:** player of sexual games, prostitute

80. **of sale:** i.e., who is for **sale**

81–82. **of such resort:** i.e., to which people come for such purposes (See picture below.)

83. **parts:** qualities, attributes

84. **principal:** employer

A house of prostitution. (4.6.79–82; 5 Chor. 1)
From [Nicholas Goodman,] *Hollands leaguer* . . . (1632).

MARINA I desire to find him so, that I may worthily
   note him.
BAWD Next, he's the governor of this country and a
   man whom I am bound to.   55
MARINA If he govern the country, you are bound to him
   indeed, but how honorable he is in that I know
   not.
BAWD Pray you, without any more virginal fencing,
   will you use him kindly? He will line your apron   60
   with gold.
MARINA What he will do graciously, I will thankfully
   receive.
LYSIMACHUS, ⌈*coming forward*⌉ Ha' you done?
BAWD My lord, she's not paced yet. You must take some   65
   pains to work her to your manage.—Come, we will
   leave his Honor and her together. Go thy ways.
                     ⌈*Bawd, Pander, and Bolt exit.*⌉
LYSIMACHUS Now, pretty one, how long have you been
   at this trade?
MARINA What trade, sir?   70
LYSIMACHUS Why, I cannot ⌈name 't⌉ but I shall offend.
MARINA I cannot be offended with my trade. Please
   you to name it.
LYSIMACHUS How long have you been of this profession?
MARINA E'er since I can remember.   75
LYSIMACHUS Did you go to 't so young? Were you a
   gamester at five or at seven?
MARINA Earlier too, sir, if now I be one.
LYSIMACHUS Why, the house you dwell in proclaims
   you to be a creature of sale.   80
MARINA Do you know this house to be a place of such
   resort, and will come into 't? I hear say you're of
   honorable parts and are the governor of this place.
LYSIMACHUS Why, hath your principal made known
   unto you who I am?   85
MARINA Who is my principal?

87. herbwoman: literally, a woman who grows herbs (here, a woman who grows **shame and iniquity** [line 88])

91. shall not see thee: i.e., will close its eyes to your offenses

95. If put upon you: i.e., **if,** instead of being **born** to your position (line 94), you were chosen; **make . . . good:** prove **the judgment** valid

101. dearer: (1) for more money; (2) with more dire consequences; **physic:** medicine

104. meanest: most worthless

110. speech had: i.e., **speech** would have; **Hold:** wait a minute

111. Persevere: accent on second syllable

114. For . . . thoughten: i.e., as **for me,** believe

117. piece: example, exemplification

A sweating tub for the treatment of
venereal disease. (4.2.20)
From Thomas Randolph, *Cornelianum dolium . . .* (1638).

LYSIMACHUS Why, your herbwoman, she that sets
  seeds and roots of shame and iniquity. O, you have
  heard something of my power, and so stand ⌈aloof⌉
  for more serious wooing. But I protest to thee,   90
  pretty one, my authority shall not see thee, or else
  look friendly upon thee. Come, bring me to some
  private place. Come, come.

MARINA
  If you were born to honor, show it now;
  If put upon you, make the judgment good   95
  That thought you worthy of it.

LYSIMACHUS
  How's this? How's this? Some more. Be sage.

MARINA   For me
  That am a maid, though most ungentle Fortune
  Have placed me in this sty, where, since I came,   100
  Diseases have been sold dearer than physic—
  That the gods
  Would set me free from this unhallowed place,
  Though they did change me to the meanest bird
  That flies i' the purer air!   105

LYSIMACHUS   I did not think
  Thou couldst have spoke so well, ne'er dreamt thou
    couldst.
  Had I brought hither a corrupted mind,
  Thy speech had altered it. Hold, here's gold for thee.   110
  Persevere in that clear way thou goest
  And the gods strengthen thee! ⌈*He gives her money.*⌉

MARINA The good gods preserve you.

LYSIMACHUS For me, be you thoughten
  That I came with no ill intent, for to me   115
  The very doors and windows savor vilely.
  Fare thee well. Thou art a piece of virtue,
  And I doubt not but thy training hath been noble.
  Hold, here's more gold for thee. ⌈*He gives her money.*⌉
  A curse upon him, die he like a thief,   120

123. **piece:** coin

130. **under the cope:** under heaven, in all the world

131. **undo:** destroy

132. **Come your ways:** i.e., **come** along

134–35. **I must . . . execute it:** wordplay on **maidenhead** as "head of a maiden" (The wordplay is spelled out in *Romeo and Juliet* 1.1.24–27.)

142. **He:** often changed by editors to "She," but see Lysimachus's words at lines 126–27

151. **An if:** i.e., even **if**

The Fool and Death. (3.2.47)
From *Todten-Tantz . . .* (1696).

That robs thee of thy goodness! If thou dost
Hear from me, it shall be for thy good.
⌜*He begins to exit.*⌝

BOLT, ⌜*at the door*⌝ I beseech your Honor, one piece
for me.

LYSIMACHUS   Avaunt, thou damnèd doorkeeper!   125
Your house, but for this virgin that doth prop it,
Would sink and overwhelm you. Away!   ⌜*He exits.*⌝

BOLT   How's this? We must take another course with
you! If your peevish chastity, which is not worth a
breakfast in the cheapest country under the cope,   130
shall undo a whole household, let me be gelded
like a spaniel. Come your ways.

MARINA   Whither would you have me?

BOLT   I must have your maidenhead taken off, or the
common hangman shall execute it. Come your   135
way. We'll have no more gentlemen driven away.
Come your ways, I say.

Enter ⌜Bawd and Pander.⌝

BAWD   How now, what's the matter?

BOLT   Worse and worse, mistress. She has here spoken
holy words to the Lord Lysimachus!   140

BAWD   O, abominable!

BOLT   He makes our profession as it were to stink afore
the face of the gods.

BAWD   Marry, hang her up forever.

BOLT   The nobleman would have dealt with her like a   145
nobleman, and she sent him away as cold as a
snowball, saying his prayers too.

BAWD   Bolt, take her away, use her at thy pleasure,
crack the glass of her virginity, and make the rest
malleable.   150

BOLT   An if she were a thornier piece of ground than
she is, she shall be plowed.

MARINA   Hark, hark, you gods!

157. **Marry come up:** an expression of amused contempt; **dish:** dishful

158. **with rosemary and bays:** i.e., garnished as if for a feast **bays:** bay leaves

164–66. **What . . . mistress:** Editors explain these puzzling lines in various ways, some claiming that Marina poses a riddle that Bolt answers confusedly and many claiming that **enemy** means Satan. Since the interpretations do not address the specific language of the text, we consider the lines as yet unexplained.

168. **better:** surpass, excel; **in their command:** i.e., in that they are in authority (over you)

172. **Coistrel:** base fellow, knave; **Tib:** strumpet

173. **choleric fisting:** enraged beating

181. **shores:** sewers

182. **by indenture:** i.e., as an apprentice

184. **thou professest:** i.e., you do as a profession

185. **own:** i.e., claim he possessed; **a name too dear:** i.e., too valuable a reputation

A beggar on crutches. (4.6.177–79)
From August Casimir Redel, *Apophtegmata symbolica* . . . [n.d.].

BAWD She conjures. Away with her! Would she had
    never come within my doors.—Marry, hang you!— 155
    She's born to undo us.—Will you not go the way of
    womenkind? Marry come up, my dish of chastity
    with rosemary and bays! ⌜*Bawd and Pander exit.*⌝

BOLT Come, mistress, come your way with me.

MARINA Whither wilt thou have me? 160

BOLT To take from you the jewel you hold so dear.

MARINA Prithee, tell me one thing first.

BOLT Come, now, your one thing.

MARINA
What canst thou wish thine enemy to be?

BOLT Why, I could wish him to be my master, or 165
    rather, my mistress.

MARINA
Neither of these are so bad as thou art,
Since they do better thee in their command.
Thou hold'st a place for which the painèd'st fiend
Of hell would not in reputation change. 170
Thou art the damnèd doorkeeper to every
Coistrel that comes enquiring for his Tib.
To the choleric fisting of every rogue
Thy ear is liable. Thy food is such
As hath been belched on by infected lungs. 175

BOLT What would you have me do? Go to the wars,
    would you, where a man may serve seven years for
    the loss of a leg, and have not money enough in the
    end to buy him a wooden one?

MARINA
Do anything but this thou dost. Empty 180
Old receptacles, or common shores, of filth;
Serve by indenture to the common hangman.
Any of these ways are yet better than this.
For what thou professest, a baboon, could he speak,
Would own a name too dear. That the gods 185
Would safely deliver me from this place!

188. **would gain:** i.e., **would** like to profit
190. **virtues:** accomplishments
192. **doubt not but:** i.e., have no doubt that
193. **scholars:** pupils
195. **Prove:** i.e., if you **prove**
200. **honest:** chaste

The Marina-figure as a musician (in a version of the
"Apollonius of Tyre" story). (4 Chor. 7–8;
4.6.189; 5 Chor. 3–4)
From *La storia d'Appollonio di Tiro e Tarsia* . . . (1616).

Here, here's gold for thee.   ⌜*She gives him money.*⌝
If that thy master would gain by me,
Proclaim that I can sing, weave, sew, and dance,
With other virtues which I'll keep from boast,   190
And will undertake all these to teach.
I doubt not but this populous city
Will yield many scholars.

BOLT   But can you teach all this you speak of?

MARINA
Prove that I cannot, take me home again   195
And prostitute me to the basest groom
That doth frequent your house.

BOLT   Well, I will see what I can do for thee. If I can
place thee, I will.

MARINA   But amongst honest ⌜women.⌝   200

BOLT   Faith, my acquaintance lies little amongst them.
But since my master and mistress hath bought
you, there's no going but by their consent. Therefore I will make them acquainted with your
purpose, and I doubt not but I shall find them   205
tractable enough. Come, I'll do for thee what I can.
Come your ways.   *They exit.*

PERICLES,

Prince of Tyre

ACT 5

5 Chorus Gower describes Marina's success in Mytilene and tells of Pericles' ship landing on Mytilene's shores.

———————

4. **lays:** songs

5. **Deep clerks:** i.e., profoundly learned scholars; **dumbs:** silences; **neele:** an archaic spelling of *neele* (here, an embroidery needle)

7. **sisters:** i.e., is like a sister to, almost duplicates

8. **inkle:** linen thread or yarn; **twin with:** perhaps, closely resemble; or, perhaps, are colored like (i.e., **rubied,** ruby-colored)

9. **race:** family, class

14–17. **driven . . . keep:** See longer note, page 197, for the corresponding passage in Gower's *Confessio Amantis*.

19. **His:** i.e., its

20. **him:** i.e., it; **hies:** hurries

21. **supposing:** i.e., imagination

21–22. **put . . . heavy:** i.e., envision the grief-stricken

22. **this:** i.e., the stage

23. **if might:** i.e., **if** possible

24. **discovered:** shown

⌈ACT 5⌉

Enter Gower.

⌈GOWER⌉
Marina thus the brothel 'scapes, and chances
    Into an honest house, our story says.
She sings like one immortal, and she dances
    As goddesslike to her admirèd lays.
Deep clerks she dumbs, and with her neele composes   5
    Nature's own shape, of bud, bird, branch, or berry,
That even her art sisters the natural roses.
    Her inkle, silk, twin with the rubied cherry,
That pupils lacks she none of noble race,
    Who pour their bounty on her, and her gain   10
She gives the cursèd bawd. Here we her place,
    And to her father turn our thoughts again,
Where we left him, on the sea. We there him ⌈lost,⌉
    Where, driven before the winds, he is arrived
Here where his daughter dwells; and on this coast   15
    Suppose him now at anchor. The city strived
God Neptune's annual feast to keep, from whence
    Lysimachus our Tyrian ship espies,
His banners sable, trimmed with rich expense,
    And to him in his barge with fervor hies.   20
In your supposing once more put your sight
    Of heavy Pericles. Think this his bark,
Where what is done in action—more, if might—
    Shall be discovered. Please you sit and hark.
                               He exits.

5.1 Lysimachus visits Pericles' ship and sends for Marina, whose music he thinks will revive the grief-stricken king. When Marina tells her story, Pericles realizes that she is his daughter. Diana appears to Pericles in a vision and tells him to go to her temple in Ephesus.

---

1. **resolve you:** i.e., answer your question
5. **craves:** asks, requests
11. **some of worth would:** i.e., a worthy (or noble) person who wishes to
14. **aught you would:** i.e., anything you wish (to know)
20. **honoring of Neptune's triumphs:** i.e., gracing (with my presence) the public festivities for Neptune
21. **ride:** lie at anchor
23. **place:** position, office

⌜Scene 1⌝

Enter Helicanus, to him two Sailors, ⌜one from the
Tyrian ship and one from Mytilene.⌝

TYRIAN SAILOR, ⌜(*to Sailor from Mytilene*)⌝
Where is Lord Helicanus? He can resolve you.
O, here he is.—
Sir, there is a barge put off from Mytilene,
And in it is Lysimachus, the Governor,
Who craves to come aboard. What is your will?   5
HELICANUS
That he have his.   ⌜*Sailor from Mytilene exits.*⌝
          Call up some gentlemen.
⌜TYRIAN⌝ SAILOR   Ho, gentlemen, my lord calls.

Enter two or three Gentlemen.

GENTLEMAN
Doth your Lordship call?
HELICANUS   Gentlemen,   10
There is some of worth would come aboard.
I pray, greet him fairly.

Enter Lysimachus, ⌜with Lords and Sailor from Mytilene.⌝

SAILOR ⌜FROM MYTILENE, *to Lysimachus*⌝   Sir,
This is the man that can, in aught you would,
Resolve you.   15
LYSIMACHUS, ⌜*to Helicanus*⌝
          Hail, reverend sir. The gods preserve you.
HELICANUS   And you, to outlive the age I am,
And die as I would do.
LYSIMACHUS   You wish me well.
Being on shore, honoring of Neptune's triumphs,   20
Seeing this goodly vessel ride before us,
I made to it to know of whence you are.
HELICANUS   First, what is your place?
LYSIMACHUS
I am the governor of this place you lie before.

29. **prorogue:** prolong

30. **Upon what ground is:** i.e., what is the reason for; **distemperature:** mental or emotional disturbance

36. **your sight:** i.e., your seeing him

41. **mortal:** fatal

46. **maid:** maiden, young unmarried woman

48. **bethought:** thought of, remembered

49. **questionless:** unquestionably, undoubtedly

50. **chosen:** choice

51. **make . . . ports:** i.e., make him hear, force its way **through his** deafened ears (literally, batter its way **through** the **defended** city gates)

53. **all happy as the fairest:** i.e., most fortunate in being the most beautiful

54. **her fellow maid:** i.e., the young woman who is her companion

Gold being tried on a touchstone. (2.2.39)
From George Wither, *A collection of emblemes* . . . (1635).

HELICANUS　Sir, 25
　Our vessel is of Tyre, in it the King,
　A man who for this three months hath not spoken
　To anyone, nor taken sustenance
　But to prorogue his grief.

LYSIMACHUS
　Upon what ground is his distemperature? 30

HELICANUS　'Twould be too tedious to repeat,
　But the main grief springs from the loss
　Of a belovèd daughter and a wife.

LYSIMACHUS　May we not see him?

HELICANUS　You may, 35
　But bootless is your sight. He will not speak
　To any.

⌜LYSIMACHUS⌝　Yet let me obtain my wish.

⌜HELICANUS⌝
　Behold him. ⌜*Pericles is revealed.*⌝ This was a goodly
　　person, 40
　Till the disaster that one mortal ⌜night⌝
　Drove him to this.

LYSIMACHUS
　Sir king, all hail! The gods preserve you. Hail,
　Royal sir!

HELICANUS
　It is in vain; he will not speak to you. 45

LORD
　Sir, we have a maid in Mytilene,
　I durst wager would win some words of him.

LYSIMACHUS　'Tis well bethought.
　She, questionless, with her sweet harmony
　And other chosen attractions, would allure 50
　And make a batt'ry through his ⌜defended ports,⌝
　Which now are midway stopped.
　She is all happy as the fairest of all,
　And, ⌜with⌝ her fellow ⌜maid, is⌝ now upon
　The leafy shelter that abuts against 55
　The island's side.

57. **effectless:** fruitless
58. **recovery's name:** i.e., the **name** of cure
62. **Wherein . . . want:** i.e., of which **we are not** deprived through scarcity
63. **staleness:** monotony
66. **graft:** i.e., plant
67. **inflict:** afflict, assail
71. **prevented:** forestalled
74. **gallant:** fine-looking, splendid
76. **gentle kind, noble stock:** Both phrases mean wellborn descent, **noble** family.
77. **rarely:** splendidly
78. **all . . . beauty:** perhaps, (you who possess) **all** the good that inheres in **beauty**
80. **prosperous:** auspicious; **artificial:** artful; skillful
82. **physic:** medicine
87. **suffered:** permitted

A lute. (4 Chor. 25)
From Silvestro Pietrasanta, *Symbola heroica* . . . (1682).

HELICANUS
Sure, all effectless; yet nothing we'll omit
That bears recovery's name.
⌜*Lysimachus signals to a Lord, who exits.*⌝
But since your kindness
We have stretched thus far, let us beseech you   60
That for our gold we may provision have,
Wherein we are not destitute for want,
But weary for the staleness.

LYSIMACHUS   O, sir, a courtesy
Which, if we should deny, the most just God   65
For every graft would send a caterpillar,
And so inflict our province. Yet once more
Let me entreat to know at large the cause
Of your king's sorrow.

HELICANUS
Sit, sir, I will recount it to you. But see,   70
I am prevented.

⌜*Enter Lord with Marina and her companion.*⌝

LYSIMACHUS   O, here's the lady that I sent for.—
Welcome, fair one.—Is 't not a goodly ⌜presence?⌝
HELICANUS   She's a gallant lady.
LYSIMACHUS
She's such a one that, were I well assured   75
Came of a gentle kind and noble stock,
⌜I'd⌝ wish no better choice, and think me rarely wed.—
Fair one, all goodness that consists in beauty:
Expect even here, where is a kingly patient,
If that thy prosperous and artificial ⌜feat⌝   80
Can draw him but to answer thee in aught,
Thy sacred physic shall receive such pay
As thy desires can wish.
MARINA   Sir, I will use
My utmost skill in his recovery, provided   85
That none but I and my companion maid
Be suffered to come near him.

89. **prosperous:** successful

89 SD. **The Song:** The words to this **song** are not preserved in the Quarto text.

90. **Marked he:** i.e., did he pay attention to

91. **us:** The plural **us** suggests that Marina's companion accompanies the song or that they both sing.

94 SD. **pushes her away:** In Twine's novel, this rejection is quite violent, and Marina's comment at line 111 suggests that it might be violent here as well. See longer note, page 197, for the passage in Twine.

96. **invited eyes:** i.e., asked to be looked at

99. **justly:** accurately, precisely

100. **wayward Fortune:** See picture, page 172. **malign:** i.e., deal malignantly with; **state:** condition, standing

104. **awkward:** adverse; **casualties:** chances, accidents

112. **I do think so:** i.e., I agree

114–15. **What countrywoman:** i.e., **what** country are you from

LYSIMACHUS   Come, let us
  Leave her, and the gods make her prosperous.
      ⌜*Lysimachus, Helicanus and others move aside.*⌝
⌜MARINA *sings*⌝

         The Song.

LYSIMACHUS, ⌜*coming forward*⌝
  ⌜Marked⌝ he your music?   90
MARINA   No, nor looked on us.
LYSIMACHUS, ⌜*moving aside*⌝
  See, she will speak to him.
MARINA, ⌜*to Pericles*⌝   Hail, sir! My lord, lend ear.
PERICLES   Hum, ha!   ⌜*He pushes her away.*⌝
MARINA   I am a maid, my lord,   95
  That ne'er before invited eyes, but have
  Been gazed on like a comet. She speaks,
  My lord, that may be hath endured a grief
  Might equal yours, if both were justly weighed.
  Though wayward Fortune did malign my state,   100
  My derivation was from ancestors
  Who stood equivalent with mighty kings.
  But time hath rooted out my parentage,
  And to the world and awkward casualties
  Bound me in servitude. ⌜*Aside.*⌝ I will desist,   105
  But there is something glows upon my cheek,
  And whispers in mine ear "Go not till he speak."
PERICLES
  My fortunes—parentage—good parentage,
  To equal mine! Was it not thus? What say you?
MARINA
  I said, my lord, if you did know my parentage,   110
  You would not do me violence.
PERICLES   I do think so.
  Pray you turn your eyes upon me.
  ⌜You're⌝ like something that—What
    ⌜countrywoman?⌝   115
  Here of these ⌜shores?⌝

118. **mortally brought forth:** i.e., born as mortals are born (The phrase carries the inevitable reminder that the birth was mortal to Thaisa.)

120. **great:** (1) filled; (2) pregnant; **deliver:** (1) give forth in words; (2) give birth

125. **pace:** gait, motion

126. **Juno:** queen of the Roman gods

132. **bred:** brought up, educated

133. **Endowments:** i.e., accomplishments; **to owe:** i.e., by possessing

135. **disdained in the reporting:** i.e., that should be scorned even while they are being told

138. **Modest:** moderate, well-conducted

140. **credit thy relation:** believe your report

142. **friends:** family, relatives (also at line 159)

MARINA   No, nor of any ⌐shores.⌐
  Yet I was mortally brought forth, and am
  No other than I appear.
PERICLES
  I am great with woe, and shall deliver weeping.   120
  My dearest wife was like this maid, and such
  A one my daughter might have been: my queen's
  Square brows, her stature to an inch;
  As wandlike straight, as silver-voiced; her eyes
  As jewel-like, and cased as richly; in pace   125
  Another Juno; who starves the ears she feeds
  And makes them hungry the more she gives them
    speech.—
  Where do you live?
MARINA   Where I am but a stranger.   130
  From the deck you may discern the place.
PERICLES
  Where were you bred? And how achieved you these
  Endowments which you make more rich to owe?
MARINA
  If I should tell my history, it would seem
  Like lies disdained in the reporting.   135
PERICLES   Prithee, speak.
  Falseness cannot come from thee, for thou lookest
  Modest as Justice, and thou seemest a palace
  For the crownèd Truth to dwell in. I will believe thee
  And make ⌐my⌐ senses credit thy relation   140
  To points that seem impossible, for thou lookest
  Like one I loved indeed. What were thy friends?
  Didst thou not ⌐say,⌐ when I did push thee back—
  Which was when I perceived thee—that thou cam'st
  From good descending?   145
MARINA   So indeed I did.
PERICLES
  Report thy parentage. I think thou said'st
  Thou hadst been tossed from wrong to injury,

150. **opened:** made known, revealed

155. **considered:** i.e., when **considered**

155–56. **the thousand . . . endurance:** i.e., a thousandth of what I have endured

158–59. **smiling . . . act:** perhaps, subduing violence with a smile **Extremity:** violence, extreme intensity **act:** the process of doing; action

181–82. **fairy / Motion:** i.e., supernatural show **Motion:** literally, a puppet show

183. **wherefore:** why

P A T I E N Z A.

"Patience." (5.1.157–59)
From Cesare Ripa, *Iconologia . . .* (1603).

And that thou thought'st thy griefs might equal mine,
If both were opened.   150
MARINA   Some such thing I said,
And said no more but what my thoughts
Did warrant me was likely.
PERICLES   Tell thy story.
If thine considered prove the thousand part   155
Of my endurance, thou art a man, and I
Have suffered like a girl. Yet thou dost look
Like Patience gazing on kings' graves and smiling
Extremity out of act. What were thy friends?
How lost thou ⌜them?⌝ Thy name, my most kind   160
   virgin,
Recount, I do beseech thee. Come, sit by me.
                                              ⌜*She sits.*⌝

MARINA   My name is Marina.
PERICLES   O, I am mocked,
And thou by some incensèd god sent hither   165
To make the world to laugh at me!
MARINA   Patience, good sir,
Or here I'll cease.
PERICLES   Nay, I'll be patient.
Thou little know'st how thou dost startle me   170
To call thyself Marina.
MARINA   The name
Was given me by one that had some power—
My father, and a king.
PERICLES   How, a king's daughter?   175
And called Marina?
MARINA   You said you would believe me.
But not to be a troubler of your peace,
I will end here.
PERICLES   But are you flesh and blood?   180
Have you a working pulse, and are no fairy
Motion? Well, speak on. Where were you born?
And wherefore called Marina?

190. **Delivered:** related

197. **give o'er: give** over, cease

199. **give me leave:** i.e., grant me permission (to ask you the following)

200. **bred:** brought up

204. **drawn:** i.e., **drawn** his sword

207. **Whither . . . me:** perhaps, what is it you want me to say or do?

211. **be:** i.e., is alive

"Wayward Fortune." (5.1.100)
From [Robert Recorde,] *The castle of knowledge* . . . [1556].

MARINA　　　　　　　　　　　Called Marina
　For I was born at sea.　　　　　　　　　　　　　185
PERICLES　　　　　　At sea? What mother?
MARINA
　My mother was the daughter of a king,
　Who died the minute I was born,
　As my good nurse Lychorida hath oft
　Delivered weeping.　　　　　　　　　　　　　190
PERICLES　　　　　　　O, stop there a little!
　⌈*Aside.*⌉ This is the rarest dream that e'er ⌈dull⌉ sleep
　Did mock sad fools withal. This cannot be
　My daughter, buried.—Well, where were you bred?
　I'll hear you more, to the bottom of your story,　　195
　And never interrupt you.
MARINA
　You scorn. Believe me, 'twere best I did give o'er.
PERICLES
　I will believe you by the syllable
　Of what you shall deliver. Yet give me leave:
　How came you in these parts? Where were you bred?　200
MARINA
　The King my father did in Tarsus leave me,
　Till cruel Cleon with his wicked wife
　Did seek to murder me; and having wooed a villain
　To attempt it, who, having drawn to do 't,
　A crew of pirates came and rescued me,　　　　205
　Brought me to Mytilene—But, good sir,
　Whither will you have me? Why do you weep?
　It may be you think me an impostor.
　No, good faith.
　I am the daughter to King Pericles,　　　　　210
　If good King Pericles be.
⌈PERICLES⌉　　　　　　　Ho, Helicanus!
HELICANUS　Calls my lord?
PERICLES
　Thou art a grave and noble counselor,

216. **is like to be:** i.e., she might **be**

222. **demanded:** asked

225. **present:** immediate

229. **beget'st, beget:** wordplay on **beget** as "to call into being" and "to father"

236. **did ever sleep:** i.e., were laid to rest forever

242. **Is . . . more:** i.e., does it require nothing **more**

Thetis. (4.4.40)
From Geoffrey Whitney, *A choice of emblemes* . . . (1586).

Most wise in general. Tell me, if thou canst,   215
What this maid is, or what is like to be,
That thus hath made me weep.
HELICANUS   I know not;
But here's the regent, sir, of Mytilene
Speaks nobly of her.   220
LYSIMACHUS   She never would tell
Her parentage. Being demanded that,
She would sit still and weep.
PERICLES
O, Helicanus! Strike me, honored sir.
Give me a gash, put me to present pain,   225
Lest this great sea of joys rushing upon me
O'erbear the shores of my mortality
And drown me with their sweetness.—O, come hither,
Thou that beget'st him that did thee beget,
Thou that wast born at sea, buried at Tarsus,   230
And found at sea again!—O, Helicanus,
Down on thy knees! Thank the holy gods as loud
As thunder threatens us. This is Marina.—
What was thy mother's name? Tell me but that,
For truth can never be confirmed enough,   235
Though doubts did ever sleep.
MARINA
First, sir, I pray, what is your title?
PERICLES
I am Pericles of Tyre. But tell me now
My drowned queen's name, as in the rest you said
Thou hast been godlike perfect, the heir of kingdoms,   240
And another ⌈life⌉ to Pericles thy father.
MARINA
Is it no more to be your daughter than
To say my mother's name was Thaisa?
Thaisa was my mother, who did end
The minute I began.   245

250. **When:** whereupon; and then

260. **sure:** assuredly, undoubtedly

263. **music of the spheres:** harmonious sound produced by the crystalline **spheres** carrying the stars and planets in the Ptolemaic system of astronomy, **music** that humankind was said no longer to be able to hear (See picture below.) **List:** listen

264. **cross:** contradict; **way:** i.e., free scope

268. **nips:** perhaps, overpowers, compels

271–72. **answer . . . belief:** i.e., correspond to **my** well-founded **belief**

272. **remember:** reward

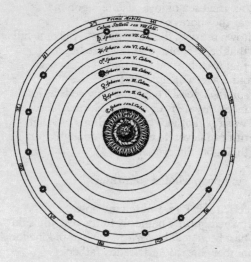

The Ptolemaic system. (1.2.130; 5.1.263)
From Marcus Manilius, *The sphere of . . .* (1675).

PERICLES
 Now, blessing on thee! Rise. Thou'rt my child.—
 Give me fresh garments.—Mine own Helicanus,
 She is not dead at Tarsus, as she should
 Have been, by savage Cleon. She shall tell thee all,
 When thou shalt kneel, and justify in knowledge 250
 She is thy very princess. Who is this?

HELICANUS
 Sir, 'tis the Governor of Mytilene,
 Who, hearing of your melancholy state,
 Did come to see you.

PERICLES, ⌜*to Lysimachus*⌝ I embrace you.— 255
 Give me my robes.—I am wild in my beholding.
      ⌜*They put fresh garments on him.*⌝
 O heavens bless my girl! But hark, what music?
 Tell Helicanus, my Marina, tell him o'er
 Point by point, for yet he seems to ⌜doubt,⌝
 How sure you are my daughter.—But what music? 260

HELICANUS My lord, I hear none.

PERICLES None?
 The music of the spheres!—List, my Marina.

LYSIMACHUS
 It is not good to cross him. Give him way.

PERICLES Rarest sounds! Do you not hear? 265

LYSIMACHUS
 Music, my lord? I hear—

PERICLES   Most heavenly music.
 It nips me unto list'ning, and thick slumber
 Hangs upon mine eyes. Let me rest. ⌜*He sleeps.*⌝

LYSIMACHUS
 A pillow for his head. So, leave him all. 270
    ⌜*Lysimachus and others begin to exit.*⌝
 Well, my companion friends, if this but answer
 To my just belief, I'll well remember you.
      ⌜*All but Pericles exit.*⌝

273. **Ephesus:** See note to 3.2.48.

275. **maiden priests:** i.e., virgin priestesses

278. **crosses:** afflictions, adversities; **call:** cry out

280. **Or . . . or:** i.e., either . . . **or**

281. **happy:** i.e., (you will live) in happiness; **silver bow:** appropriate to **Diana** as goddess of hunting and of the moon (See picture below.)

284. **Goddess argentine:** i.e., silvery **goddess**

287. **My purpose was for:** i.e., I had purposed (resolved) to go to

290. **blown:** full; **Eftsoons:** soon afterward

291. **refresh us:** i.e., **refresh** ourselves

The goddess Diana (2.5.9, 10; 3.2.120; 3.3.33; 4 Chor. 4; 4.2.153; 5.1.272 SD, 283)

From Robert Whitcombe, *Janua divorum* . . . (1678).

Diana ⌜*descends.*⌝

DIANA
My temple stands in Ephesus. Hie thee thither
And do upon mine altar sacrifice.
There, when my maiden priests are met together,   275
Before the people all,
Reveal how thou at sea didst lose thy wife.
To mourn thy crosses, with thy ⌜daughter's,⌝ call,
And give them repetition to the ⌜life.⌝
Or perform my bidding, or thou livest in woe;   280
Do 't, and happy, by my silver bow.
Awake, and tell thy dream.   ⌜*She ascends.*⌝
PERICLES   Celestial Dian,
Goddess argentine, I will obey thee.—
Helicanus!   285

⌜*Enter Helicanus, Lysimachus, Marina, and
Attendants.*⌝

HELICANUS   Sir.
PERICLES
My purpose was for Tarsus, there to strike
The inhospitable Cleon, but I am
For other service first. Toward Ephesus
Turn our blown sails. Eftsoons I'll tell thee why.—   290
Shall we refresh us, sir, upon your shore,
And give you gold for such provision
As our intents will need?
LYSIMACHUS   Sir,
With all my heart. And when you come ashore,   295
I have another ⌜suit.⌝
PERICLES   You shall prevail
Were it to woo my daughter, for it seems
You have been noble towards her.
LYSIMACHUS
Sir, lend me your arm.   300
PERICLES   Come, my Marina.
                                    They exit.

5.2 Gower tells of the celebrations for Pericles in Mytilene and of the betrothal of Marina and Lysimachus.

———

1. **sands, run:** The image is of the sand in an hourglass. (See picture, page 114.)
2. **More . . . dumb:** i.e., (I'll tell) **a little more** (of the story) and **then** be silent
3. **my last boon:** i.e., the **last** favor I shall ask
5. **aptly:** readily; suitably
9. **So he thrived:** i.e., Lysimachus **thrived so** well
12. **Till he:** i.e., until Pericles
14. **confound:** bring to nothing
15. **feathered briefness:** Proverbial: "Time has wings." (See picture, page 122.)
16. **fall out:** come to pass, turn out
20. **by . . . doom:** i.e., through the discernment of **your** imaginations, for which I am **thankful**

5.3 At Diana's temple in Ephesus, Thaisa recognizes Pericles as her husband and is reunited with him and with her daughter.

———

1. **just:** exact; or, full

⌜Scene 2⌝

⌜*Enter Gower.*⌝

GOWER
Now our sands are almost run,
More a little, and then dumb.
This my last boon give me—
For such kindness must relieve me—
That you aptly will suppose   5
What pageantry, what feats, what shows,
What minstrelsy and pretty din
The regent made in Mytilene
To greet the King. So he thrived
That he is promised to be wived   10
To fair Marina, but in no wise
Till he had done his sacrifice
As Dian bade, whereto being bound,
The interim, pray you, all confound.
In feathered briefness sails are filled,   15
And wishes fall out as they're willed.
At Ephesus the temple see
Our king and all his company.
That he can hither come so soon
Is by your fancies' thankful doom.   20
⌜*He exits.*⌝

⌜Scene 3⌝

⌜*Enter Cerimon and Diana's Priestesses, including
Thaisa; at another door enter Pericles, Marina,
Helicanus, Lysimachus, and Attendants.*⌝

PERICLES
Hail, Dian! To perform thy just command,
I here confess myself the King of Tyre,
Who, frighted from my country, did wed

7. **Wears ... livery:** i.e., still **wears** the **livery** of the goddess of chastity, is still a virgin

8. **nursed with:** i.e., brought up by

9. **her better stars:** i.e., planets with a more favorable influence over her life (in astrological thought)

10. **'gainst whose shore riding:** i.e., (as our ship was) lying at anchor just off Mytilene's **shore**

11. **fortunes:** luck, fate

12. **remembrance:** memory

14. **favor:** appearance, face

20. **Reverend appearer:** i.e., you who appear worthy of reverence

27. **recovered:** revived

33. **let me look:** See longer note, page 198.

34. **none of mine:** i.e., not my husband

The Destinies or Fates. (1.2.116; 3.3.9; 4.3.14)
From Vincenzo Cartari, *Imagines deorum* ... (1581).

At Pentapolis the fair Thaisa.
At sea in childbed died she, but brought forth   5
A maid child called Marina, whom, O goddess,
Wears yet thy silver livery. She at Tarsus
Was nursed with Cleon, who at fourteen years
He sought to murder. But her better stars
Brought her to Mytilene, 'gainst whose shore riding,   10
Her fortunes brought the maid aboard us, where,
By her own most clear remembrance, she made known
Herself my daughter.

THAISA   Voice and favor!
You are, you are—O royal Pericles!   15
                            ⌐*She falls in a faint.*⌐

PERICLES
What means the ⌐nun?⌐ She dies! Help, gentlemen!

CERIMON   Noble sir,
If you have told Diana's altar true,
This is your wife.

PERICLES   Reverend appearer, no.   20
I threw her overboard with these very arms.

CERIMON
Upon this coast, I warrant you.

PERICLES   'Tis most certain.

CERIMON
Look to the lady. O, she's but overjoyed.
Early ⌐one⌐ blustering morn this lady was   25
Thrown upon this shore. I oped the coffin,
Found there rich jewels, recovered her, and placed her
Here in Diana's temple.

PERICLES   May we see them?

CERIMON
Great sir, they shall be brought you to my house,   30
Whither I invite you. Look, Thaisa
Is recoverèd.   ⌐*Thaisa rises.*⌐

THAISA   O, let me look!
If he be none of mine, my sanctity

35. **bend:** incline
36. **spite of seeing:** i.e., no matter what I see
45. **parted:** departed from

The triumph of Time. (2.3.49)
From Francesco Petrarca, *Opera* . . . [1508].

Will to my sense bend no licentious ear,   35
But curb it, spite of seeing.—O, my lord,
Are you not Pericles? Like him you spake,
Like him you are. Did you not name a tempest,
A birth and death?
PERICLES   The voice of dead Thaisa!   40
THAISA
That Thaisa am I, supposèd dead
And drowned.
PERICLES ⌜Immortal⌝ Dian!
THAISA   Now I know you better.
                    ⌜*She points to the ring on his hand.*⌝
When we with tears parted Pentapolis,   45
The king my father gave you such a ring.
PERICLES
This, this! No more, you gods! Your present kindness
Makes my past miseries sports. You shall do well
That on the touching of her lips I may
Melt and no more be seen.—O, come, be buried   50
A second time within these arms!   ⌜*They embrace.*⌝
MARINA, ⌜*kneeling*⌝   My heart
Leaps to be gone into my mother's bosom.
PERICLES
Look who kneels here, flesh of thy flesh, Thaisa,
Thy burden at the sea, and called Marina   55
For she was yielded there.
THAISA, ⌜*embracing Marina*⌝ Blessed, and mine own!
HELICANUS
Hail, madam, and my queen.
THAISA   I know you not.
⌜PERICLES⌝
You have heard me say, when I did fly from Tyre   60
I left behind an ancient substitute.
Can you remember what I called the man?
I have named him oft.
THAISA   'Twas Helicanus then.

73. **resolve:** answer
75. **officer:** agent
77. **relives:** lives anew
83. **thy vision:** i.e., the **vision** in which you appeared to me
84. **night oblations:** i.e., nightly prayers
87. **ornament:** an ironic reference to his uncut hair
88. **Makes:** i.e., that **makes; to form:** i.e., into the proper shape
89. **what . . . touched:** i.e., his face
91. **credit:** authority
93. **there:** i.e., in **Pentapolis** (line 86)

PERICLES Still confirmation!   65
  Embrace him, dear Thaisa. This is he.
                                ⌜*They embrace.*⌝
  Now do I long to hear how you were found,
  How possibly preserved, and who to thank,
  Besides the gods, for this great miracle.
THAISA Lord Cerimon, my lord, this man   70
  Through whom the gods have shown their power,
    that can
  From first to last resolve you.
PERICLES   Reverend sir,
  The gods can have no mortal officer   75
  More like a god than you. Will you deliver
  How this dead queen relives?
CERIMON   I will, my lord.
  Beseech you, first go with me to my house,
  Where shall be shown you all was found with her,   80
  How she came placed here in the temple,
  No needful thing omitted.
PERICLES
  Pure Dian, ⌜I⌝ bless thee for thy vision, and
  Will offer night oblations to thee.—Thaisa,
  This prince, the fair betrothèd of your daughter,   85
  Shall marry her at Pentapolis.—And now this
    ornament
  Makes me look dismal will I clip to form,
  And what this fourteen years no razor touched,
  To grace thy marriage day I'll beautify.   90
THAISA
  Lord Cerimon hath letters of good credit, sir,
  My father's dead.
PERICLES
  Heavens make a star of him! Yet there, my queen,
  We'll celebrate their nuptials, and ourselves
  Will in that kingdom spend our following days.   95
  Our son and daughter shall in Tyrus reign.—

97. **we do our longing stay:** i.e., **we** postpone (the fulfilling of) **our** desires

98. **untold:** i.e., which is (as yet) **untold**

Epilogue Gower reflects on the now-completed story and tells the fate of Cleon and Dionyza.

---

5. **fell:** cruel

10. **charity:** kindness, benevolence; **aye:** always

John Gower.
From George Wilkins, *Pericles prince of Tyre*
(1608; facsimile title page, 1857).

Lord Cerimon, we do our longing stay
To hear the rest untold. Sir, lead 's the way.
⌜*They exit.*⌝

⌜EPILOGUE⌝

⌜*Enter Gower.*⌝

GOWER
  In Antiochus and his daughter you have heard
  Of monstrous lust the due and just reward.
  In Pericles, his queen, and daughter seen,
  Although assailed with fortune fierce and keen,
  Virtue ⌜preserved⌝ from fell destruction's blast,   5
  Led on by heaven, and crowned with joy at last.
  In Helicanus may you well descry
  A figure of truth, of faith, of loyalty.
  In reverend Cerimon there well appears
  The worth that learnèd charity aye wears.   10
  For wicked Cleon and his wife, when fame
  Had spread his cursèd deed ⌜to⌝ the honored name
  Of Pericles, to rage the city turn,
  That him and his they in his palace burn.
  The gods for murder seemèd so content   15
  To punish, although not done, but meant.
  So on your patience evermore attending,
  New joy wait on you. Here our play has ending.
⌜*He exits.*⌝

Longer Notes

1.2.38. till you return to us: This is one of several puzzling lines in this scene—one of the most incoherent in a text that, overall, has significant problems with coherence and language. For example, the dialogue between Pericles and Helicanus—lines 40–72—is given no narrative context: Helicanus refers to a "Signior Sooth [i.e., Sir Flattery] here" (line 47), but no one in the scene has flattered Pericles; Helicanus's begging for forgiveness and Pericles' anger seem equally unmotivated.

2.1.103–4. Pentapolis: While the other cities featured in *Pericles*—Tyre, Antioch, Tarsus, Mitylene, and Ephesus—are easily located along the coast of the eastern Mediterranean (as well as on maps of St. Paul's journeys), the location of Pentapolis remains unresolved. As Linda McJannet writes, "there were seven Pentapolises known in the ancient world." Many scholars and editors would equate Shakespeare's Pentapolis with the one that is near (or the same as) Cyrene, found on the northern coast of Africa. (See, e.g., Suzanne Gossett, ed., *Pericles*, The Arden Shakespeare, 3rd ed. [2004], p. 129.) McJannet argues that such a location does not accord with the action described in the play, where Pericles and Thaisa, sailing from Pentapolis to Tyre, are blown by a wind from the north to the waters off Ephesus. Were Pentapolis in Africa, a south wind would have been needed. She suggests two possibilities among the seven ancient Pentapolises and makes a persuasive case for one, the city of Tomi on the coast of the Black

Sea and thus to the north of Ephesus. Such a location would accord not only with the tempest from "the grizzled North" that "drives" "the poor ship" (3 Chor. 47–50), but also with the description of the storm hitting the ship when it was halfway through its journey from Pentapolis to Tyre (3 Chor. 45–46).

Yet McJannet herself acknowledges that Cnidus, an island near Rhodes, is also a possibility. And noting, on a map of St. Paul's journeys, a group of five cities "on or near the northern coast of the Aegean whose names end in '-polis,'" she acknowledges that Shakespeare might have thought of that set of five cities as corresponding to Twine's and Gower's "Pentapolis." Thus, though we find McJannet's case for Tomi persuasive, the argument remains too speculative for us to assign that location to Pentapolis on our map of the play's geography, page xii. (See Linda McJannet, "Genre and Geography: The Eastern Mediterranean in *Pericles* and *The Comedy of Errors*," in *Playing the Globe: Genre and Geography in English Renaissance Drama*, ed. John Gillies and Virginia Mason Vaughan [Madison, N.J.: Fairleigh Dickinson University Press; London: Associated University Presses, 1998], pp. 86–106, esp. 91, 95–96.)

2.1.162. **This jewel . . . arm:** This line is traditionally explained by editors as referring to Pericles' armor, but we agree with Gossett's proposal that it instead refers to a jeweled bracelet that has remained on Pericles' arm. Such a reading makes sense of the speech as a whole: The sailors have furthered Pericles' recovery of the armor (line 160); the jeweled bracelet has remained on his **arm** and will serve to buy the **courser** of lines 163–65. (See Gossett, ed., *Pericles*, p. 239.)

2.2.59. **The outward habit by the inward man:** The book inscribed with the quotation from "Shackesphere" is Chapman's *A Pleasant Comedy intituled Humerous dayes Myrth,* 1599 (STC 4987 copy 1). The volume was acquired by Mr. Folger at the Sotheby sale of "The Dramatic Library of Percy Fitzgerald Esq." on Friday, June 14, 1907. On the reverse of the last leaf is written "Thomas Bentley owe[ns] this book; he is a foole that scans the Inward habitts by the outwarde man. **Shackesphere.**" This reading of the inscription is that of Laetitia Yeandle, the Folger's Manuscript Curator Emerita, who dates the hand to the mid–seventeenth century. The Folger has not determined the identity of Thomas Bentley. We are grateful to Laetitia Yeandle and to Betsy Walsh, Head of Readers' Services, for providing this information.

2.4.10. **for they so stunk:** During the third and second centuries B.C.E., there were four kings of Syria named Antiochus. John Gower (and Shakespeare following him) attributes the building of Antioch to the third Antiochus, Antiochus the Great (who ruled Syria from 223 to 187), though historians today date its founding closer to the time of the first King Antiochus in the third century B.C.E. The fourth King Antiochus, who features in the apocryphal 2 Maccabees, is Antiochus Epiphanes, who ruled Syria from 175 to 164 and who tried to destroy Judaism. In 2 Maccabees 9.5–10, this king, like the Antiochus in *Pericles*, is struck down by heaven for his offenses while seated in his chariot. The biblical king was "carried violently" from his chariot to the ground, worms came from his body, and his flesh fell off. Shakespeare's fictional king is destroyed by a fire from heaven. Both kings, though, "so stunk" that their previously admiring subjects turned from them in horror. In *Pericles*, "all those eyes adored them, ere their fall, / Scorn now their hand should give them burial." In 2 Maccabees, "the filthiness of his smell was noisome to all his army. Thus no man could bear, because of his stink, him that a little afore thought he might reach to the stars of heaven." Shakespeare perhaps checked the name "Antiochus" in the index to the Geneva Bible (the Bible he most often used), which would have led him directly to this passage in 2 Maccabees.

3.1.72. **coffin:** The words *coffer* and *coffin* are usually distinguished by Shakespeare, with *coffer* meaning a chest for jewels or money and *coffin* meaning a chest for burying a dead body. In this play, the words are often confused. See 3.4.2, e.g., where *coffer* refers to Thaisa's coffin.

3.2.36–40. **secret art . . . stones:** Cerimon's description of his expertise as a physician recalls such books as *The book of secrets of Albertus Magnus of the virtues of herbs, stones, and certain beasts . . .* , first translated into English in 1550, and reprinted many times during the sixteenth and early seventeenth centuries. Such "books of secrets" deal with the marvelous properties (some real, some imagined) of "**vegetives, . . . metals, stones.**" In *The book of secrets,* several healing remedies from "vegetives" involve infusions from plants (e.g., the "juice" of the daffodil is prescribed for pain of the kidneys or the legs, and the juice of the plantain is prescribed for dysentery). Infusions from stones are said to be created by breaking such stones as "Medius" (probably a mixture of metallic sulphates) and dissolving them in water to create remedies for the gout or blindness, and by breaking Memphis stone (probably dolomite) and mixing it with water to produce a painkiller. (See *The Book of Secrets of Albertus Magnus of the Virtues of Herbs, Stones and Certain Beasts . . .* , ed. Michael

R. Best and Frank H. Brightman [Oxford: Clarendon Press, 1973].)

Cerimon's use of the phrase **"secret art,"** while probably carrying the primary meaning of "learning known only to a few," also suggests a link between his practice of **"physic"** and what was called "natural magic," defined by Giambattista della Porta as "this wonderful **Art"** and "the perfect knowledge of natural things." Della Porta, in his *Natural Magick ... wherein are set forth all the Riches and Delights of the Natural Sciences* (published in Italian in 1558 and translated into English in 1658), says that a "magician" must also be a "skillful Physician" knowing "mixtures and temperatures," as well as a "Herbalist," "skillful and sharp-sighted in the nature of all plants." "The knowledge of plants is so necessary to this profession," he writes, "that indeed it is all in all. He must be as well seen [i.e., learned] also in the nature of Metals, Minerals, Gems and Stones."

3.2.47. To please the fool and death: This line is too opaque to paraphrase, but its general sense seems to be that since wealth is transitory, only **the fool** would value it, and that **death,** which separates a man from his wealth, would take pleasure in the **"silken bags"** because the wealthier the man, the more **death** can mock him. It has been suggested that there may be an allusion here to the figures of **Death** and **the Fool** in the Dance of Death tradition pictured on page 150.

3.2.102. viol: Editors do not agree whether this word should be **viol** or "vial." Those who print "vial" argue that a vial of medicine is more appropriate to the scene. We follow Q in printing **viol** because the word occurs in the middle of a three-line passage calling for music. An audience would presumably be unable to detect from the sound of the word which spelling had been chosen, though stage action could support either.

3.4.9. **vestal:** Vesta, in Roman religion, was the powerful goddess of the hearth. In her temple in Rome, virgin priestesses (vestals) tended the sacred fire. Any vestal who lost her virginity was punished by being buried alive. In *Pericles*, the word *vestal* is almost synonymous with "virgin," but in 3.4 it also seems linked to the famous Ephesian Temple of Artemis or Diana; it is possible that the virgins who in mythology attend on Artemis/Diana and whose virginity is jealously guarded by the goddess became confused with the virgin priestesses of Vesta.

4.4.40. **Thetis:** In classical mythology, Thetis is the name of a sea goddess; but in poetry, in confusion with Tethys, the wife of Oceanus, she often personifies the sea itself.

4.6.13. **greensickness:** As Gail Kern Paster explains, this "illness" in young women (originally thought to be a menstrual disorder) was also called "the virgin's disease" and "virgin's melancholy." It was characterized by listlessness, pallor, and aversion to food. Paster, who links this supposed "illness" to what she calls "virginal reluctance," studies a variety of Shakespearean and other characters in drama of the period who exemplify beliefs about its characteristics and its cure. (See Gail Kern Paster, "Love Will Have Heat: Shakespeare's Maidens and the Caloric Economy," in her *Humoring the Body: Emotions and the Shakespearean Stage* [Chicago: University of Chicago Press, 2004], pp. 77–134, esp. 89ff.)

5 Chor. 14–17. **driven . . . keep:** In Gower's version
of the tale, the hero's arrival in Mitylene and the city's
celebration of Neptune are described as follows:

And thus tofore the wynd thei dryue,
Til longe and lat they arryue
With great distresse, as it was sene
Upon this towne of Mytelene,
Whiche was a noble cite tho [i.e., city then].
And happeneth thylke [i.e., at this same] tyme so
The lordes bothe, and the commune [i.e., common
   people]
The high festes of Neptune
Upon the stronde at ryvuage [i.e., on the shore at
   the coast],
As it was custome and vsage,
Solempnelych they be sight [i.e., solemnly they cele-
   brated].
   Gower's *Confessio Amantis* (1532), book 8, fol. 183r

5.1.94 SD. **pushes her away:** In Twine's novel, this
incident appears as follows:

Then Apollonius fell in a rage, and forgetting all
courtesie, his vnbridled affection stirring him
thereunto, rose vp sodainly, and stroke the maiden
on the face with his foote, so that shee fell to the
ground, and the bloud gushed plentifully out of
her cheekes. And like it is that shee was in a
swoone, for so soone as shee came to her selfe,
shee beganne to weepe, saying: O immortall God
which madest heauen and earth, looke vppon my
afflictions, and take compassion vppon mee. I was
borne among the waues and troublesome tempests
of the sea[.] (1594, sig. I 2v)

5.3.33. let me look: Gossett suggests, in commenting on this line, that the play assumes that priestesses of Diana's temple were subject to the same rules that governed nuns in Roman Catholic convents, rules that would have forbidden the nun to look directly at a man. Such a suggestion is persuasive, especially since it makes good sense of lines 34–36. (See Gossett, ed., *Pericles*, page 399.)

Textual Notes

The reading of the present text appears to the left of the square bracket. Unless otherwise noted, the reading to the left of the bracket is from **Q**, the First Quarto text (upon which this edition is based). The earliest sources of readings not in **Q** are indicated as follows: **Q2** is the Second Quarto of 1609; **Q4** is the Fourth Quarto of 1619; **Q6** is the Sixth Quarto of 1635; **F3** is the Third Folio of 1663–64; **F4** is the Fourth Folio of 1685; **Ed.** is an earlier editor of Shakespeare, beginning with Rowe in 1709. (We have taken no readings from the Third Quarto of 1611 or from the Fifth Quarto of 1630.) No sources are given for emendations of punctuation or for corrections of obvious typographical errors, like turned letters that produce no known word. **SD** means stage direction; **SP** means speech prefix; *uncorr.* means the first or uncorrected state of the First Quarto; *corr.* means the second or corrected state of the First Quarto; ~ stands in place of a word already quoted before the square bracket; ʌ indicates the omission of a punctuation mark.

1 Chorus 1. SP GOWER] Ed.; *omit* Q   11. these] Q2; those Q   17. then:] ~ ʌ Q   39. a] F3; of Q

1.1 18. razed] Ed.; racte Q   25. boundless] Ed.; bondlesse Q   57. blow.] Ed.; blow (*Antiochus*) Q   58. SP ANTIOCHUS Scorning] Ed.; Scorning Q   61, 62. 'sayed] Q (sayd)   64. advice] Q (aduise)   102. clearʌ] ~: Q   103. them.] ~, Q   110. fit,] ~; Q   117. our] F3; your Q   119. cancel] F3; counsell Q   126. SD *All . . . exit.*] Q (*Manet Pericles solus.*)   133. you're] F3; you Q   142. 'schew]

199

Ed.; shew Q   168. SD *Enter a Messenger.*] *1 line earlier in* Q   171. SP ANTIOCHUS] *Antin.* Q   179. SP ANTIOCHUS Thaliard, adieu] Ed.; *Thaliard* adieu Q

1.2   0. SD *with an Attendant*] Ed.; *with his Lords* Q   2. change] Q (chãge)   4. Be my] Ed.; By me Q   6. should] stould Q   16. care;] ~∧ Q   19. me. The] ~∧ ~ Q   23. him] Ed.; *omit* Q   28. th' ostent] Ed.; the stint Q   33. am] Ed.; once Q   44. wind] Ed.; sparke Q   46. err.] ~, Q   49. pardon] paadon Q   54. Helicanus] *Hellicans* Q   66. heaven] heauẽ Q   74. me∧] ~: Q   77. Where, as] Q (Whereas)   90. me] Ed.; *omit* Q   91. fears] F4; feare Q   93. doubt] Ed.; doo't Q   99. call 't] Ed.; call Q   104. from] Q (frõ)   130. we'll] Ed.; will Q   132. SD *They exit.*] Q (*Exit.*)

1.3   0. SD *alone*] Q (*solus*)   1. SP THALIARD] *omit* Q   3. 'Tis] t'is Q   18. depart,] ~? Q   18–19. you. | Being at Antioch—] ~, . . . ~. Q   29. ears it] Ed.; seas Q   32. SP HELICANUS] Q4; *omit* Q   35. betook] Q2; betake Q   40. SD *They exit.*] Q (*Exit*)

1.4   5. aspire∧] ~? Q   13. do] Q2; to Q   13. deep∧] ~: Q   14. do] Ed.; to Q   14. weep∧] ~. Q   14. lungs] Ed.; toungs Q   15. Fetch] feteh Q   33. 'tis] t'is Q   37. they] Q2; thy Q   40. two savors] Q (too sauers)   68. Hath] Ed.; That Q   70. men] Ed.; mee Q   71. glory's] Q (glories)   75. him's] Q (himnes)   78. fear?] Q4; leaue∧ Q   79. The] Q4; our Q   79. lowest,] ~? Q   107. ne'er] Q (neare)

2 Chorus   1. SP GOWER] Ed.; *omit* Q   11. Tarsus] Q4, Q (*Tharstill*)   12. speken] Q (spoken)   17. Helicane] Q (*Helicon*)   22. Sends word] Ed.; Sau'd one Q   24. had intent to murder] Q *corr.;* hid in Tent to murdred Q *uncorr.*   25. Tarsus] Q (*Tharsis*)   31. unquiet] vnqiuet Q   32. safe∧] ~; Q

2.1   1. heaven!] ~, Q   12. What ho,] Ed.; What, to Q   12. Pilch] Q (pelch)   17. thee] Q ('th)   33. devours] Ed.; deuowre Q   41. SP THIRD FISHERMAN] Ed.; I.

Q   50. finny] Ed.; fenny Q   81. quotha] Q (ke-tha)
82. gown.] ∼∧ Q   85. holidays] Ed.; all day Q   86.
moreo'er] Ed.; more; or Q   94. your] Q4; you Q   103.
is] Q2; I Q   111. Marry] Q (Mary)   120. wife's] Q
(Wiues)   120. SD *net*] *Ne1* Q   125. pray] Q *corr.*; pary
Q *uncorr.*   126. yet] Q *corr.*; yeat Q *uncorr.*   126. thy]
Ed.; *omit* Q   132. brace] Q (brayse)   133. it.] ∼∧ Q
134. from] Ed.; Fame Q   134. may 't] Ed.; may Q
152. do 'ee] Q *corr.*; di 'e Q *uncorr.*   153. on 't] Q (an't)
154. 'twas] t'was Q   157. you'll] Q *corr.* (you'le); you le
Q *uncorr.*   162. biding] Ed.; buylding Q   164. delight-
ful] F3; delight Q

  2.2 0. SD *Attendants*] Q (*attendaunce*) 1 *and
throughout.* SP SIMONIDES] Ed.; *King.* Q   29. what's]
Ed.; with Q   31. chivalry] Chiually Q   32. *pompae*] Q
(*Pompey*)   48. From] Q (frō)   55. furnishèd] Q (fur-
nisht)

  2.3 3. To] Ed.; I Q   13. yours] Ed.; your Q   20.
Marshal] Q (Martiall)   41. Yon] Ed.; You Q   47. son's]
Ed.; sonne Q   54. stored] Ed.; stur'd Q   103. 'twas]
t'was Q   111. SD *They dance.*] *1 line later in* Q   120. SP
SIMONIDES] Ed.; *omit* Q

  2.4 13. 'Twas] T'was Q   23. welcome.] ∼∧ Q   36.
death's] Ed.; death Q

  2.5 17. 'Tis] T'is Q   76. SD *Aside*] *After line 77* Q
78. you, not∧] ∼∧∼, Q   80. SD *Aside*] *After line 81* Q
88. destroy.] ∼, Q   94. SP BOTH] Q (*Ambo.*)

  3 Chorus 1. SP GOWER] Ed.; *omit* Q   7. crickets]
Ed.; Cricket Q   10. Where, by] Ed.; Whereby Q   13.
eche] Q (each)   17. coigns] Ed.; Crignes Q   21. stead]
Q (steed)   21. quest.] ∼∧ Q   23. To th'] Q (To' th)   34.
Pentapolis] *Penlapolis* Q   35. Y-ravishèd] Iranyshed Q
41. cross?] ∼∧ Q   51. and, well-anear] ∼∧∼ Q   57.
not∧ . . . told.] ∼? . . . ∼, Q   58. hold∧] ∼: Q   60. sea-
tossed] Ed.; seas tost Q

  3.1 8. spit] Q (speat)   10. Unheard.] ∼∧ Q   11. pa-

troness] patrionesse Q   11. midwife] Ed.; my wife Q
47. Slack] Q *corr.;* Slake Q *uncorr.*   47. bowlines] Q
(bolins)   56. custom] Ed.; easterne Q   57–58. yield 'er,
for she must overboard straight] Ed.; yeeld 'er Q   59.
meet.—Most] Ed.; meet; for she must ouer board
straight: | Most Q   65. the ooze] Ed.; oare Q   67. And
e'er-remaining] Ed.; The ayre remayning Q   70. paper]
Q2; Taper Q   75. chest] Q (Chist)   77. thee, mariner.]
~: ~ˌ Q   86. SD *They exit.*] Q (*Exit.*)

3.2 0. SD *two Suppliants*] This ed.; *a seruant* Q   4.
'T has] Q (T'as)   5. SP FIRST SUPPLIANT] This ed.; *Seru.*
Q   6. ne'er] Q (neare)   22, 35, 60, 62, 64, 65. 'Tis] T'is
Q   53 SD, 57. *chest,* chest] Q (*Chist*)   66. bitumed]
Ed.; bottomed Q   70. open.] ~ˌ Q   77. too!] Ed.; to ˌ
Q   86. *requite*] Q (*requit*)   91. looks.] ~ˌ Q   97. lain]
Q (lien)   99. cloths] Q (clothes)   105. warm] Ed.;
warmth Q   118. weepˌ] ~. Q   126. to,] ~ˌ Q   128.
SD *They . . . exit.*] Q (*They carry her away. Exeunt
omnes.*)

3.3 0. SD *at Tarsus*] Q (*Atharsus*)   34. Unscis-
sored] Ed.; vnsisterd Q   35. ill] Ed.; will Q   42. o' th']
Q (ath)   43. masked] Q (mask'd)

3.4 0. SD *Thaisa*] Tharsa Q   5. bearing] Ed.; learning Q   9. vestal] Q (vastall)   11. SP CERIMON] *Cler.* Q
16. SP THAISA] *Thin.* Q   17. SD *They exit*] Q (*Exit*)

4 Chorus 1. SP GOWER] *omit* Q   4. there 's] ther's Q
8. music] Ed.; Musicks Q   10. high] Q (hie)   14.
Seeks] Ed.; Seeke Q   17. ripe] Q2; right Q   17. rite]
Ed.; sight Q   21. sleided] Q (sleded)   25. to the] Q
(too'th)   26. bird] Ed.; bed Q   29. Dian,] ~ˌ Q   32.
With] Ed.; *omit* Q   32. might the] Ed.; might with the
Q   44. wrathˌ] ~. Q   47. carry] Ed.; carried Q

4.1 5. thy bosom] Ed.; thy loue bosome Q   16.
strew] Q (strowe)   21. as] Ed.; *omit* Q   26. me!] ~? Q
28. O'er the sea marge] Ed.; ere the sea marre it Q   34.
servant] Q (seruãt)   44. complexion] eomplexion Q

52. said] Q (sed)   62. nurse] nutse Q   62. says] Q (ses)
71. "Ha!" says] Q (ha ses)   83–84. killed? | Now,] ~ʌ~?
Q   87. la] Q (law)   90. for 't] Q (fort)   100. life.] ~ʌ Q
100. Come you] ~, ~ Q   107. SD *They . . . Marina.*] Q
(*Exit*)

4.2   0. SD *Pander, Bawd, and Bolt*] F3; *the three
Bawdes* Q   4. much] Ed; much much Q   27. chequins]
Q (Checkins)   34. 'twere] t'were Q   43. SP PIRATE] Ed.;
Sayler Q   54. presently] presenly Q   65. struck] Q
(strooke)   67. had but] Ed.; had not Q   77. pleasure]
peasure Q   87. Marry] Q (Marie)   108. i' the] Q (ethe)
124. lovers.] ~ʌ Q   130. SP BAWD] F3; *Mari.* Q   154.
you?] ~ʌ Q   155. SD *They exit.*] Q (*Exit.*)

4.3   1. are] Q4; ere Q   4. child] chidle Q   6. A] Ed.;
O Q   8. o' th'] Q (ath)   11. 't had] Q (tad)   14. Fates.]
~ʌ Q   15. is] Ed.; it Q   30. prime] Ed.; prince Q   35.
distain] Ed.; disdaine Q   37. Marina's] Q (Marianas)
38. malkin] Q (Mawkin)   39. through] Q (thorow)
49. golden] Q (goldē)   54. Seize] Q (ceaze)   54.
talons] Q (talents)   55. You're] Q (Yere)   56. to the] Q
(too'th)   56. flies] Fliies Q

4.4   2. for 't] Q (fort)   8. in the] Ed.; with Q   8.
youʌ] ~. Q   9. story.] ~ʌ Q   10. the] Ed.; thy Q   12.
life's] Q (liues)   13. along.] ~ʌ Q   14. mind,] ~. Q
16. high] Q (hie)   18. his] Ed.; this Q   19. go on] Ed.;
grone Q   20. gone.] ~ʌ Q   23. See] Ed.; *Gowr.* See Q
27. o'ershowered,] ~. Q   30. puts] Ed.; put Q   30. sea.
He bearsʌ] ~ʌ ~ ~, Q   32. witʌ] ~: Q   40. o' th'] Q
(ath')   48. orderèdʌ] ~; Q   49. scene] Ed.; Steare Q
50. welladayʌ] ~. Q

4.5   9. SD *They exit.*] Q (*Exit.*)

4.6   0. SD *Bawd, Pander, and Bolt*] Ed.; *Bawdes 3* Q
15. SD *Enter Lysimachus.*] *3 lines later in* Q   21. to-
bless] Q (to blesse)   23. may so.] ~, ~ʌ Q   23, 31.
'Tis] t'is Q   38. dignifies] Q4; dignities Q   65. paced] Q
(pac'ste)   71. name 't] F3; name Q   89. aloof] Ed.;

aloft Q 135. common hangman] Q (cõmon hãg-man)
137. SD *Bawd and Pander*] Ed.; *Bawdes* Q 144. Marry]
Q (*Marie*) 157. womenkind] wemen-kinde Q 172.
Coistrel] Q (custerell) 200. women] Q4; woman Q

5 Chorus 1. SP GOWER] Ed.; *omit* Q 8. silk,
twin∧] ~∧~, Q 8. twin] Q (Twine) 10. pour] Q
(powre) 13. lost] Ed.; left Q 20. fervor] Q *corr.* (fer-
uor); former Q *uncorr*

5.1 1. SP TYRIAN SAILOR] Ed.; 1.*Say.* Q 2. is.] ~∧ Q
8. SP TYRIAN SAILOR] Ed.; 2.*Say.* Q 9. SP GENTLEMAN] Q
(1.*Gent.*) 13. SP SAILOR FROM MYTILENE] Ed.; I.*Say.* Q
corr.; Hell. Q *uncorr.* 16. reverend] Q (reuerent) 32.
from] Q (frõ) 36. bootless∧] ~. Q 36. sight. He] Q
corr. (sight, hee); sight∧ see, Q *uncorr.* 37. any.] Ed.;
any, yet let me obtaine my wish. Q 38. SP LYSIMACHUS
Yet . . . wish.] Ed.; *Lys.* Behold him, this was a goodly
person. Q 39–41. SP HELICANUS Behold . . . | Till] Ed.;
Hell. Till Q 41. night] Ed.; wight Q 51. defended] Q2;
defend Q 51. ports] Ed.; parts Q 54. with] Ed.; *omit* Q
54. maid, is] Ed.; maids Q 70. SP HELICANUS] *Holl.* Q
72. here's] hee'rs Q 73. presence] Ed.; present Q 77.
I'd] Q4; I do Q 77. wed] Ed.; to wed Q 78. one] Q (on)
80. feat] Ed.; fate Q 89. SP MARINA] Ed.; *omit* Q 90.
Marked] Q4; Marke Q 104. awkward] augward Q
114. You're] Ed.; your Q 115. countrywoman] Q6;
Countrey women Q 116. Here] Q (heare) 116, 117.
shores] Ed.; shewes Q 125. cased] Q (caste) 138.
palace] Q (*Pallas*) 139. crownèd] Q (crownd) 140.
my] Q4; *omit* Q 143. say] Ed.; stay Q 149. thought'st]
Q (thoughts) 160. them] Ed.; *omit* Q 181–82. fairy∧ |
Motion?] ~? ~∧ Q 192. dull] Ed.; duld Q 195. to the]
Q (too'th) 208. impostor] Q (imposture) 212. SP PERI-
CLES] Ed.; *Hell.* Q 215. wise in general.] ~; ~~, Q
237. First] Frist Q 241. life] Ed.; like Q 246. Thou'rt]
Q (th'art) 257. music?] ~∧ Q 259. doubt,] Ed.; doat.
Q 279. life] Ed.; like Q 296. suit] Ed.; sleight Q

5.2 8. Mytilene∧]~. Q 9. King.] ~, Q 12. sacri-
fice∧] ~. Q 14. pray you] ~, ~ Q 15. filled] F3; Q
(fild) 16. willed] F3; Q (wild) 17. see∧] ~, Q

5.3 16. nun] Ed.; mum Q 20. Reverend] Q
(Reuerent) 25. one] Ed.; in Q 43. Immortal] Q4; I,
mortall Q 60. SP PERICLES] F3; *Hell.* Q 64. 'Twas]
T'was Q 74. Reverend] Q (Reuerent) 82. needful]
needfulll Q 83. I] Ed.; *omit* Q 91. credit,] ~. Q 98.
SD *They exit.*] Q4 (*Exeunt.*); *FINIS.* Q

Epilogue 4. keen,] ~. Q 5. preserved] Ed.;
preferd Q 12. to] Ed.; *omit* Q 15. seemèd] Q
(seemde) 18. ending.] ending. | FINIS. Q

Appendix: The "Pericles" Story in Gower and Twine

When Gower, speaking as the play's Chorus, says that he is simply repeating the story he read in his sources ("I tell you what mine authors say" [1 Chor. 20]), he reminds us that the story dramatized in *Pericles* had been available in manuscript and in print for centuries (though, as Gower does not point out, with a hero named Apollonius rather than Pericles). That the Chorus speaks in the person of Gower also reminds the reader or audience that a version of the "Pericles" story is included in one of John Gower's major works.

Gower's fourteenth-century *Confessio Amantis* (or "The Lover's Confession," which, despite its Latin title, is in English) contains in its eighth book the lengthy story of the trials and tribulations of Apollonius of Tyre. This story, the primary source for *Pericles*, is itself a rewriting of one of the world's most popular tales. First written in about the third century C.E.—perhaps in Latin, perhaps in Greek—the *Historia Apollonii* is extant today in more than a hundred Latin manuscripts, the earliest of which are from the ninth century; there also exist an eleventh-century Anglo-Saxon translation and thirteenth-century manuscripts in Danish, Old French, Spanish, and Norse. John Gower, in adapting the story in the early 1390s, had several manuscript versions on which to draw. Though his narrator cites Godfrey of Viterbo's twelfth-century *Pantheon* as his authority for the Apollonius story, the *Confessio* actually draws details from several other versions as well, including the Latin *Gesta Romanorum* and an eleventh-century text in Latin prose.

Just as John Gower drew on multiple written authorities in crafting his version of the Apollonius story, so too did the author of *Pericles*. The Apollonius story went from manuscript into print almost as soon as printing began in Europe—as early as 1470 in Latin, 1471 in German, and 1483 in English—and by the time *Pericles* was written (probably in late 1607 or early 1608), several versions of the story had been printed and reprinted in English. Gower's *Confessio Amantis* was printed by Caxton in 1483, and reprinted in 1532 and again in 1554. Sometime before 1576, Laurence Twine translated a French version of the story as it appeared in the *Gesta Romanorum;* the resulting novel, *The Patterne of Painefull Aduentures*, was printed in 1594 and reprinted in 1607.

There can be little doubt that the *Confessio Amantis* is the primary authority for *Pericles*. The very verse form in which the Chorus generally speaks—iambic tetrameter couplets—was used by John Gower, and at most points the story aligns itself with that recounted in the *Confessio Amantis*. As scholars have long known, however, several scenes in *Pericles* pull in material from Twine's novel. It was from Twine, for example, that the black-comic brothel scenes were drawn. In its weaving of material from the *Confessio Amantis* with that from Twine, *Pericles* combines two of the major exemplars of the Apollonius story—one that descended through Godfrey of Viterbo to Gower and the other through the *Gesta Romanorum* to Twine.

Some scholars believe that George Wilkins's 1608 novel, *The Painefull Aduentures of Pericles Prince of Tyre,* should be considered as a source for the play, even though Wilkins advertises his book as an account of "the Play of *Pericles*" "as it was . . . by the Kings Maiesties Players excellently presented." Many scholars today also argue that Wilkins wrote much of *Pericles*.

For our explanation of why we have difficulty accepting this claim, see "An Introduction to This Text," pages liii–liv. (For a more detailed explanation, see Barbara Mowat, " 'I tell you what mine Authors saye': *Pericles, Shakespeare*, and *Imitatio*," *Archiv* 240 [2003]: 42–59. For more on the Apollonius story and its transmission in manuscript and print, see Elizabeth Archibald, *Apollonius of Tyre: Medieval and Renaissance Themes and Variations, Including the Text of the Historia Apollonii Regis Tyri with an English Translation* [Cambridge: D. S. Brewer, 1991], esp. pp. 3, 7–9, 45–50, 183–90.)

Pericles: A Modern Perspective

Margaret Jane Kidnie

Pericles is a play haunted by loss. Sometimes loss is figured as a sudden and calamitous separation from one's friends and belongings, as when Pericles at the top of the second act is washed ashore after a shipwreck at sea, hungry and cold, or when Thaisa, Pericles' wife, wakes from death to find herself alone in a strange country. At other moments, loss is evoked through the death, or seeming death, of a close family member or friend. Pericles mourns his wife, and later his daughter, Marina; Marina, in turn, early brought on stage as a newborn, makes her first entrance as an adult in Act 4, grieving the death of her nurse, Lychorida. For Marina, as for the rest of her family, the world seems "a lasting storm, / Whirring me from my friends" (4.1.21–22).

In Shakespeare's tragedies, death tends to function as a terminus. Death may be shocking—one thinks of Romeo and Juliet killing themselves in the Capulet tomb, or King Lear bearing onstage the body of hanged Cordelia—but it imposes on the plot a sense of finality and closure. Yet the romances, among which *Pericles* is typically numbered, work to a different effect. Works in this genre, a troubling blend of comedy and tragedy to which Shakespeare turned late in his career, look beyond death to its painful aftermath. Thus in plays such as *Pericles, The Tempest, Cymbeline,* and *The Winter's Tale,* death comes early and produces not "silence," as Hamlet would have it, but desire.

In *Pericles,* this desire takes the form of a deep longing for the recovery of what has been lost. Such intense longing can bring with it danger, as we see in the play's opening episodes, set in the nightmarish fairy-tale kingdom of Antioch. "This king unto him took a peer [wife]," Gower tells us, "Who died and left a female heir . . . With whom the father liking took" (1 Chor. 21–25). Antiochus's daughter, the woman who finds identity solely through an abusive relationship with her male parent, fills the rupture caused by her mother's death by becoming both daughter and wife to her father/husband. The perversity of Antiochus's solution to family loss is signaled in the riddle he devises to deter his daughter's potential suitors. It registers images of corrupt appetite alongside a bewildering conflation of familial relations:

> I am no viper, yet I feed
> On mother's flesh which did me breed.
> I sought a husband, in which labor
> I found that kindness in a father.
> He's father, son, and husband mild;
> I mother, wife, and yet his child.
> How they may be, and yet in two,
> As you will live resolve it you.

$$(1.1.66–73)$$

If Pericles answers the riddle correctly, he is promised a royal wife through whom he might propagate his own issue (1.2.78–79); if he fails to solve it, he forfeits his life. This device, an implicit test of singularity and virtue, is familiar to spectators from ancient Greek legend, folktale, and even Shakespeare's earlier *Merchant of Venice*. The challenge for Pericles, however, lies not in unraveling the riddle but in delivering its answer. The domestic arrangement that makes sense of the conundrum is "incest," and the "I" of the riddle (whether the verse is spoken in performance by Antiochus, Pericles, or Antiochus's daughter) is the near-silent daughter, the object and prize of the contest. The answer to the riddle is self-evident, yet literally unspeakable. The fact that the daughter's name is never revealed points at once to the king's crime and to the personal and cultural trauma of a family that "feed[s]" on itself. The name that functions as the key to the riddle is thus an absence or gap in the narrative that neither Pericles nor the theater audience can provide.

Family lineage, naming, identity, and the desires prompted by loss—themes linked in such a startling manner at Antioch—shape the scenes that follow. But not everything that is lost remains beyond recovery, nor does every act of surrogacy carry with it the horror of incest. In seeking a wife, for example, Pericles is also seeking a father (more precisely, a father-in-law) to stand in place of his own dead father. He "would be son to great Antiochus," he explains in a moment of intense dramatic irony before attempting the riddle (1.1.27). Later, symbolically clad in his father's armor—a token of his heritage lost to him through shipwreck, but fortuitously pulled from the sea—he finds in King Simonides at the court of Pentapolis "my father's picture" (2.3.41). His marriage to Simonides' daughter, Thaisa, is thus framed by a memory of personal loss. Pericles gains at Pentapolis both wife and father, repairing generational absence through reproductive family alliances.

But this moment of parental substitution in Pentapolis also carries within it echoes of its incestuous double, since the situation in significant ways replays the circumstances of the opening episode in Antioch. Each kingdom is ruled by a male parent with a single female heir, and each king hosts a competition in which knights, hopeful of marriage, seek honor. The ceremonial procession of knights and shields at Pentapolis, with its spectacular display of cryptic visual emblems and mottos, is reminiscent of the murderous riddle witnessed at Antioch. Even more remarkably, despite commending his daughter's choice of husband and affirming to himself that he "will no longer / Have it [their marriage] be delayed," Simonides then inexplicably decides he "must dissemble" his favor (2.5.20–22). Realist theater accounts for this sudden plot complication with difficulty, as Simonides is given no motivation for his actions. However, the function of this fleeting intrusion of the vision of an angry father and the threat of entrapment is less realist than symbolic. It summons onstage a former time of fear and horror precisely in order to dispel it. This moment in which Pericles seems to find Antioch reappearing in Pentapolis (2.5.44–45) acts as a corrective to incestuous relations by transforming them, as though by magic, into orderly marriage and the birth of Marina.

Thus, despite an evidently straightforward linear structure that tends to move from one self-contained episode to the next by means of either a marked shift in fictional location or an imagined passage of years, *Pericles* evinces a subtle pattern of repetition and doubling that creates an ever-stronger sensation of strange, even uncanny, recurrence. The action follows the hero's adventures around the eastern Mediterranean, with the story branching into three independent threads when in the third act Pericles, his wife, and daughter are separated at sea. For Shakespeare's audience, place-names such as Tyre, Tarsus, Antioch, and Mytilene would have conjured up foreign, ancient, and perhaps also specifically non-Christian settings. Modern scholars, however, are unable to determine with certainty whether Pentapolis refers to a city, or a group of five cities, on the southern coast of Asia Minor or on the north coast of Africa. This late romance—not unlike *The Winter's*

Tale, a play that notoriously gives landlocked Bohemia a seacoast—depends for its effect not on geographical precision but on a rather more vague and associative sense of location.

Moreover, as is true of many plays performed on the early modern stage, settings "out there" are simultaneously "right here." The fishermen, for example, whom Pericles encounters when he washes up on the shores of Pentapolis, talk in familiar English terms about "rich misers" who "never leave gaping till they swallowed the whole parish" (2.1.30–35), describe beggars "whipped" by the "beadle" (96–97), and allude to abuses of the legal system (121–22)—all topical social issues extensively debated by Elizabethan and Jacobean morality writers. The brothel into which Marina is sold, with its lecherous Spanish and diseased French clients bringing with them both money and infection (4.2.102–16), likewise dramatizes recognizably English prejudices and circumstances.

Narrative continuity is imposed on a story that sprawls over multiple regions and a temporal period of more than fourteen years through the device of the Chorus. "To sing a song that old was sung, / From ashes ancient Gower is come" (1 Chor. 1–2). "Ancient Gower"—the first character to take the stage—shepherds spectators across the seas and through the years, introducing and commenting on place, time, and character (1 Chor.); shifting the action among locations and plots (4 Chor.); and reporting, sometimes by means of dumb show, events that fall between episodes (3 and 4 Chor.). John Gower, an English poet, retold in the fourteenth century a version of the story that Shakespeare, perhaps with a collaborator, picked up more than two hundred years later and transformed into a play. This popular story of the adventures of Pericles (originally Apollonius) of Tyre was ancient even when Gower told it in book 8 of his *Confessio Amantis*. As Chorus to the play, Gower thus knowingly tells the theater audience once again a story he himself has taken from "mine authors" (1 Chor. 20), and with which he assumes they are already familiar. *Pericles*, as we have seen, is deeply preoccupied with family legacy in terms of inheritance, memory, and lineage. On another level, the story itself forms part of a cultural legacy, told and so passed down to generations of auditors and spectators.

Gower's many intrusions into the drama remind us that the tale is art—"his story," and not "history." Gower's peculiar relation to the action as its self-conscious narrator is signaled through clues in the verse. The third chorus, for instance, narrates Marina's conception the night following the marriage of Pericles and Thaisa, evoking the nocturnal stillness of the household when familiar domestic spaces, occupied by human bustle during the day, are given over during the hours of sleep to other creatures:

> Now sleep yslackèd hath the rout;
> No din but snores about the house,
> Made louder by the o'erfed breast
> Of this most pompous marriage feast.
> The cat with eyne of burning coal
> Now couches from the mouse's hole,
> And crickets sing at the oven's mouth
> Are the blither for their drouth.
>
> (3 Chor. 1–8)

Gower's verse form, vocabulary choices, and phrasal patterns would have seemed old-fashioned even to early modern theatergoers. The obsolete past participial form found in the opening line, followed by an obsolete plural form in the vivid description of the "cat with eyne of burning coal," makes him sound archaic,

out of place and time. This effect of archaism is reinforced through both the use of iambic tetrameter (a
four-foot line, in place of the more usual five-foot line)
and the heavy predominance of rhyming couplets.
Gower sounds, fittingly enough, like the medieval author he is, fully belonging neither to the world of his
tale nor to the world of his auditors.

One challenge for a modern production of *Pericles* is
to identify a context able to accommodate the way
Gower is both part of, yet distanced from, the adventures of Pericles and his family. The BBC-Time/Life tel-
evision production tries to replicate Gower's own
historical moment, suggesting his medieval origins
through costuming choices and verbal accent. Another
response, which was especially popular in twentieth-
century theater, is to modernize the role. Productions
of *Pericles* staged in recent years at the Stratford Festi-
val of Canada and at the Royal Shakespeare Company
in Britain have variously presented Gower as an Afro-
Caribbean storyteller, as a female gospel singer (with
the choruses transformed into song), and as a dancer
in the style of Japanese butoh, dressed in a loincloth
and white body paint, his verse accompanied by heavily stylized movement. These stage treatments in effect
find modern analogues that can make accessible to
modern spectators the medieval oral tradition out of
which the character of Gower emerges.

The story is Gower's, yet it remains a question to
whom or what the play's qualified happy ending should
be attributed. *Pericles* dramatizes irresistible forces
that operate beyond human will and control. These
forces—variously described as the "gods" or "Fortune"—are capricious. They give and they take away,
seemingly without reason. Their potential for both
good and ill is neatly illustrated when Pericles loses his
father's armor in the shipwreck, only to regain it unex-

pectedly when the fishermen haul up their nets
(2.1.124). When Thaisa, much later, seems to die in
childbirth, the grieving Pericles reproaches the gods,
asking, "Why do you make us love your goodly gifts /
And snatch them straight away?" (3.1.25–26). But Fortune's wheel continues to turn, eventually transforming
even this adversity into good. The goddess Diana appears to Pericles in a vision, redirecting him and his
ship to her temple at Ephesus, and it is through this in-
tercession that Thaisa is finally reunited with her husband and daughter. "Now I know you better," she says,
correctly identifying a token that, like a dead father's
armor in another place and another time, forms part of
Pericles' heritage: "When we with tears parted Pentapolis, / The king my father gave you such a ring"
(5.3.44–46). Thaisa, buried by her husband at sea in
Act 3, is found alive at the end of Act 5, then "buried / A
second time within [his] arms" (5.3.50–51).

But the accident that initiates Pericles' recovery first
of the dead Marina, then of the dead Thaisa—specifically, what brings him to the shores of Mytilene and thus
near his unknown daughter—is never explained. It
might be interpreted as coincidence, unacknowledged
divine intervention, or even the invisible hand of the
omniscient storyteller, guiding his tale to a comic resolution. The storms of earlier acts are stilled, replaced by
the mental storm and danger of bodily shipwreck that
Pericles embraces upon learning of his daughter's supposed death: "He swears / Never to wash his face nor cut
his hairs. / He puts on sackcloth, and to sea. He bears / A
tempest which his mortal vessel tears, / And yet he rides
it out" (4.4.28–32). His condition of despair prompts the
city's governor, Lysimachus, himself reformed by Marina's virtue, to summon a maid to speak to a king.

Their encounter is filled with dramatic irony. The
theater audience, but nobody on stage, knows that

each of these characters has the ability to remedy a key loss suffered by the other. This, alongside an acute awareness that they might part ways without ever discovering their familial relation, generates a suspense that makes almost unbearably painful the power of the moment of their mutual recognition. These characters come to each other as ciphers. The silent Pericles is obliquely identified by Helicanus in terms of his ship: "Our vessel is of Tyre, in it the King" (5.1.26). Marina is introduced by Lysimachus simply as "the lady that I sent for" (72), one who, we later learn, when questioned about her parentage, "would sit still and weep" (221–23). The situation is reminiscent of the circumstances of Antiochus's daughter, whose mother's trauma-causing death leads to the daughter's disturbing erasure of personal identity. Struck by her mention of "wayward Fortune" (100), "ancestors / Who stood equivalent with mighty kings" (101–2), and "parentage" rooted out by time (103), the nameless king finally looks at the nameless woman standing before him: and what he sees is the image of his dead wife. This is a deeply troubling moment. In an important sense, *Pericles* never entirely escapes the preoccupation with incest first introduced at Antioch. The dangers summoned up by a man who finds a wife in his child are then reinforced by echoes of that much earlier riddle of identity. "What countrywoman? / Here of these shores?" he asks, to which she cryptically answers, "No, nor of any shores. / Yet I was mortally brought forth, and am / No other than I appear" (114–19).

The resolution of this paradox is one of many answers Pericles must seek before he can finally believe that this woman—a woman with his daughter's name who looks exactly like his wife—is truly the lost Marina. As the scene moves toward reunion, he identifies himself as "Pericles of Tyre" (238), and thus Marina's father. It is at this moment that the king, surrounded by witnesses, pauses to demand of Marina the third name that, still unheard, has yet haunted the scene. When Marina speaks the name of her mother, the process of recovery is complete: "Is it no more to be your daughter than / To say my mother's name was Thaisa? / Thaisa was my mother, who did end / The minute I began" (242–45). The sophisticated dramaturgy of this scene, especially the way it delays its revelations by so carefully withholding answers to which the audience is already privy, creates for spectators as a theatrical effect the intensity of the characters' desire to recover what has been lost.

Pericles enacts the desire to defeat death, an almost mythic objective in keeping with the play's resolutely nonrealist content. Not only does a goddess appear to Pericles in a vision—a true *dea ex machina*—but there are other hints of the supernatural, as when Marina decides to remain with the silent and potentially violent royal stranger because "something glows upon my cheek, / And whispers in mine ear 'Go not till he speak'" (5.1.106–7). Such circumstances set aside as irrelevant any objection to seeming glitches in the narrative. How, for instance, is Thaisa, lodged at the temple of Diana at Ephesus, able to receive news of her father's death through "letters of good credit" sent to Lord Cerimon (5.3.91–92), yet unable in a period of more than fourteen years to communicate either with Pentapolis or Tyre to tell her family she did not die at sea? Thaisa's continued absence from the tale is driven by the logic of the play's narrative. Brought back to life either by magic or art, Thaisa remains dead to Gower's story until she is recovered from the convent by her husband and daughter, thereby regaining both her identity within that family and her former place in the narrative as wife and mother. Such a sequence of events is not plausible outside of the theater, but neither are returns from death. *Pericles* dramatizes not what we know will happen but what we wish could happen. Even in fantasy, however, the ending is tinged with sadness. The characters never get back the lost years, and some deaths are irreversible—surely the point of learning of Simonides' death in the play's closing moments. In place of the sort of comic resolution typical of, say, *As You Like It* or *A Midsummer Night's Dream, Pericles* offers a bittersweet tale of suffering and loss eventually brought to a close with the achievement of a qualified happiness.

The final scene is remarkable as the only moment in the play in which the theater audience sees a family composed of two parents and a child. This same familial organization was potentially available at Tarsus, but significantly, Philoten, the daughter of Cleon and Dionyza, never appears onstage. These parents are thus primarily judged as foster parents to Marina, the dangers of surrogacy foregrounded through Dionyza's criminal decision to murder her charge. The recurrence of parents and children in Antioch, Pentapolis, Tarsus, and Ephesus makes evident the play's interest in diverse models of parental authority. What is perhaps less obvious is a parallel concern with rule as it relates to state affairs. The conception of the king-as-father guiding his subjects-as-children was a commonplace of early modern, especially Jacobean, political theory. This identification of the private with the public accounts for Pericles' otherwise baffling decision to separate his family once again at the very moment they achieve reunion, sending the newly found Marina to govern with Lysimachus in Tyre, while he and Thaisa travel to Pentapolis. It also implies that parents such as Antiochus, Simonides, Cleon, and Dionyza should be understood and interpreted as models of government. Cleon and Dionyza are thus not just wicked (foster) parents but wicked governors, a conclusion seemingly reinforced by Gower's description of the people rising up in "rage" to burn them in their palace, the gods in this instance likewise "content / To punish [murder], although not done, but meant" (Epilogue 13, 15–16). Worthy fathers and kings, Gower's closing chorus implies, enjoy peaceable, happy reigns and a secure succession; others, such as the incestuous Antiochus, are literally destroyed by the avenging fires of heaven (2.4.9–10).

Spectators, even while comforted by Gower's editorial moralizing, might perceive oversights and inconsistencies suggesting that the dangers of parenting and rule are rarely so easily or safely avoided. The fishermen's extended commentary on the rule of King Simonides, for example, a "good" king who nevertheless governs a state in which "the great ones eat up the little ones" (2.1.29–30), points to some of the injustices that defeat even strong and well-loved leaders. The wished-for happy ending cannot entirely dispel problems encountered over the course of the play; and while deep desires prompted by loss are eventually fulfilled, the possibility of future loss remains ever-present. In particular, the vision of succession with which *Pericles* closes incorporates within itself the potential for disorder, especially as embodied in the as-yet-untested future parents of children and state. Lysimachus encountered his bride in a brothel, and while evidently transformed by her virtue and words, his rule at Mytilene, both before and after meeting Marina, is characterized by corrupt dealings, exploitation, and infection. Syphilis in Shakespeare's London, a sexually transmitted disease popularly known as the "pox," was lingering, contagious, and incurable. In the troubling figure of Lysimachus, this tragicomic romance embraces within its closing tableau the potential for still more secrets, and further riddles.

Further Reading

Pericles

Abbreviations: *Cym.* = *Cymbeline;*
Err. = *The Comedy of Errors;*
MM = *Measure for Measure; Per.* = *Pericles;*
Temp. = *The Tempest; WT* = *The Winter's Tale*

Archibald, Elizabeth. " 'Deep Clerks She Dumbs': The Learned Heroine in *Apollonius of Tyre* and *Pericles.*" *Comparative Drama* 22 (1988–89): 289–303.

Education and learning are important themes in the earliest extant version of the Apollonius of Tyre story, the basis of Shakespeare's *Pericles.* Tarsia, the counterpart to Shakespeare's Marina, preserves her chastity in a brothel by proclaiming "Habeo auxilium studiorum liberalium, perfecte erudita sum" ("I have the benefit of a liberal arts education, I am fully educated"). Subsequent versions of the story, such as Gower's *Confessio Amantis* and Laurence Twine's *Patterne of Painefull Aduentures*, also emphasize the heroine's education. Shakespeare, however, plays down Marina's intellectual skills by giving Gower only half a line on her brains, in contrast to three and a half lines on her sewing (5 Chor. 5–8). Marina herself never boasts of her education, and her encounter with Pericles in 5.1 is less intellectual and more emotional than in the earlier works. By celebrating stereotypical feminine skills— i.e., weaving, sewing, and singing—*Pericles* seems

223

more old-fashioned on the topic of female education than its medieval and Renaissance sources and analogues, thereby fitting well with Lisa Jardine's account of the "ambivalent attitudes to learned women in the Renaissance" ("Cultural Confusion and Shakespeare's Learned Heroines," *Shakespeare Quarterly* 39 [1987]: 1–18).

Barber, C. L. " 'Thou That Beget'st Him That Did Thee Beget': Transformation in *Pericles* and *The Winter's Tale.*" *Shakespeare Survey* 22 (1969): 59–67.

In Barber's psychoanalytic reading, the final recognition scenes in *Pericles* and *WT* become "epiphanies of something sacred[,] . . . arrived at by a dramatic movement" that contrasts with the trajectory of the earlier, festive comedies. In those plays, where the emotional center resides in young lovers, the movement is toward the creation of new family units; in the two romances, because the center of feeling inheres in the older generation, the action moves "through experiences of loss back to the recovery of family relations in and through the next generation." Central to Barber's thesis are the sacredness of the initial union between mother and infant and the emotional repercussions for the male protagonist of the traumatic break with the maternal. Through the recovery of the daughter, which leads to the recovery of the wife, those lost become "ikons for a pious love which finds in them the mysterious powers which create and renew life." As a result, family ties are freed from the threat of sexual degradation explicitly manifested at the outset of *Pericles* in the incestuous relationship between Antiochus and his daughter.

Brockbank, J. Philip. "*Pericles* and the Dream of Immortality." *Shakespeare Survey* 24 (1971): 105–16.

Shakespeare's late plays address the question of personal survival in a life to come by reminding us that doctrines of immortality cannot do what they are meant to do. As the last pages of Wittgenstein's *Tractatus Logico-Philosophicus* state, the "solution of the riddle of life in time and space lies outside space and time," or, put another way, "the solution to the problem of life is seen in the vanishing of the problem." Through the false deaths and miraculous resurrections of the romances, Shakespeare intimates "some solace of immortality" by way of metaphor and rhythm rather than through dogma or a conclusion reached by systematic thought. The play's informing metaphor, the sea, is elemental and the "old tale" told is "elementary. We are fashioned from the elements, we are exposed to them, and we revert to them": hence Marina's birth at sea, the many voyages, and Thaisa's apparent death. "The reawakening and restoring of the life of the affections after desolating loss is the continuing mystery, delight, preposterousness and satisfaction of [*Pericles*]," a play that reassures through its creation of a world in which "death is an illusion and the dream of immortality is appeased without the postulate of an after-life."

Greenfield, Thelma N. "A Re-Examination of the 'Patient' Pericles." *Shakespeare Studies* 3 (1968 for 1967): 51–61.
  Greenfield takes issue with critics who describe Pericles as patient, silent, and unrebellious. Thinking that the portrait of Pericles as a patient man should be supplanted by that of "a wise and learned one, the Renaissance descendant of a wily Greek traveler"—along the lines of Plutarch's Pericles, Homer's Odysseus, and Sophocles' Oedipus—Greenfield contends that Pericles reacts to the storm at 2.1.1–11 not submissively, as some have suggested, nor with imperatives like the

contentious Lear, but like a scholar disputing with the elements: "[M]an must yield to you powers of nature; I am a man; therefore I obey you." Just as he does in his encounter with Antiochus, Pericles relies on wit and retreats in the face of overwhelming odds. To those who claim that Shakespeare made Pericles less violent and therefore more patient than he appears in earlier versions of the Apollonius story, Greenfield responds that the text's lack of stage directions renders the degree of the title character's onstage grief uncertain. In short, the play emphasizes Pericles' "avoidance of and retreat from misfortunes rather than his patient endurance of them." If there is anyone in the play who demonstrates patience, it is Marina.

Healy, Margaret, "Pericles and the Pox." In *Shakespeare's Late Plays: New Readings*, edited by Jennifer Richards and James Knowles, pp. 92–107. Edinburgh: Edinburgh University Press, 1999.
Healy attends to the "medico-moral politics" of *Pericles* in order to counter critical claims that the play should be read as a retreat into pure aestheticism or a celebration of royal absolutism. In the early seventeenth century, syphilis (popularly known as the pox) was an untreatable, much feared, and highly contagious sexually transmitted disease allegorically associated in English polemic with the Church of Rome. The emphasis in the brothel scenes on the diseased bodies of the exploited sex workers suggests strongly that Lysimachus, a regular customer, is likewise contaminated. Pericles' decision to marry his daughter to the governor of Mytilene makes him appear both tyrannical and self-serving. His abuse of power as a father and king speaks in turn to the controversial efforts on the part of James VI (James I) to strengthen English diplomatic relations with Spain through the marriage of his children to the Infanta and the Duke of Savoy.

The conjunction of kingship, marriage, and syphilis in *Pericles* thus functions as an oblique criticism of English state politics in the first decade of the seventeenth century.

Helms, Lorraine. "The Saint in the Brothel: Or, Eloquence Rewarded." *Shakespeare Quarterly* 41 (1990): 319–32.

Helms traces the motif of the Prostitute Priestess (i.e., the virgin who is sent to a brothel) from the declamations of Seneca the Elder through Christian hagiography and the romance sources and analogues of *Pericles* to the play itself. In the Senecan version, the woman kills her would-be rapist, thereby setting up a forensic argument on the issue of whether the killing or even the very time spent in the brothel disqualifies her from joining the order of vestal virgins. The open structure of the declamation format, with its improvised arguments, suggests that a woman can survive the worst circumstances devised by a man. As found in the story of St. Agnes, the motif depicts a virgin protected from the brothel's customers by angels until God allows her to achieve martyrdom; the closed structure of the saint's life implies that when a woman is placed in a whorehouse, her only alternative is death. Marina, the virginal heroine of *Pericles*, resorts to neither martyrdom nor murder when brought to a brothel but instead preserves her chastity through rhetorical eloquence. Like the silence of Isabella in *MM*, another eloquent Shakespearean virgin, Marina's silence at the end of the play when marriage is imposed on her must be negotiated theatrically. That silence, which is closer to the theatrical ellipses of the Senecan declamations than to the authorial closure of narrative hagiography and romance, leads Helms to conclude that Marina "reanimates the figure of the Prostitute Priestess, as the Shakespearean playtext reenacts the Senecan rhetoric of rape."

Hillman, Richard. "Shakespeare's Gower and Gower's Shakespeare: The Larger Debt of *Pericles*." *Shakespeare Quarterly* 36 (1985): 427–37.

In his reappraisal of the Chorus, Gower, the most "sustained literary allusion in Shakespeare," Hillman claims that the importance of the *Confessio Amantis* goes beyond the story of Apollonius found in book 8. When taken as a whole, the *Confessio* forms a precedent for Shakespeare's "use of love themes as a means of exploring larger issues of human spirituality and self-realization." From Gower's first words in the play, which combine "the conquering of death and the resuming of mortality," through passages like 2 Chor. 5–8, the Chorus assures us that "transcendence is possible" and that suffering can be redemptive. Such a moral and spiritual context, within which capricious fortune is contained and a point given "to growth, change, and response," is absent from the tale of Apollonius but part of the *Confessio*'s framework, thus making it a suitable source for the first of Shakespeare's romances.

Hoeniger, F. David. "Gower and Shakespeare in *Pericles*." *Shakespeare Quarterly* 33 (1982): 461–79.

In an attempt to reconcile the poor critical reputation of *Pericles* with its success on the stage in several mid-twentieth-century revivals, Hoeniger contends that those parts of the play usually dismissed as defective and even crude were "deliberately adapted to an 'inferior art,' " and may indicate that Shakespeare is winking at his audience. In setting out to "recreate old tales" in the romances, the mature Shakespeare apparently determined that it would be desirable to begin by imitating the old-fashioned techniques of early storytellers. In the plays that followed, he would discover "ways of creating a new art entirely his own." Hoeniger finds a similarly purposeful use by an author of a style considered unworthy of him in Chaucer, who assigns himself the jingling "Rime of Sir Thopas" and follows it with the mirthless "Tale of Melibeus," two burlesque efforts that contrast with the splendid artistry of the other Canterbury Tales.

Kurland, Stuart M. " 'The Care . . . of Subjects' Good': *Pericles,* James I, and the Neglect of Government." *Comparative Drama* 30 (1996): 220–44.

Kurland examines *Pericles* in the context of early Jacobean politics. The title figure, a prince who seems uninterested in the fate of his kingdom, encounters similar royal indifference to good government in the other rulers he meets in his travels: "the incestuous and cruel Antiochus, the ineffective but kindly Cleon, the 'good Simonides' [aware of inequities in his kingdom but unable or unwilling to correct them], and the licentious but miraculously transformed Lysimachus." Pericles' travels convey an overall sense of purposelessness and drift, and his "remoteness and general passivity" mirror James I's much-observed "disinclination to stay in London . . . to govern and to be seen governing." Topical misgivings about the king's apparent indifference to the business of government animate the politics of the play. One must look to Marina, not Pericles, for "a model of initiative and principled resourcefulness."

McJannet, Linda. "Genre and Geography: The Eastern Mediterranean in *Pericles* and *The Comedy of Errors*." In *Playing the Globe: Genre and Geography in English Renaissance Drama,* edited by John Gillies and Virginia Mason Vaughan, pp. 86–106. Madison, N.J.: Fairleigh

Dickinson University Press; London: Associated University Presses, 1998.

Because of their association with myth and fairy tale, the romances, with the exception of *Temp.*, are not usually examined for Shakespeare's "handling of geography, history, or other markers of cultural otherness." Even when "real places" are involved, they are usually considered decorative, having little or no regard for geographic or historical accuracy. Despite anachronisms in *Pericles* and *Err.* (McJannet includes the latter because of its romance framing plot and the setting of Ephesus), the treatment of geography and cultural otherness in these two plays merits attention for several reasons. First, setting operates in both texts as a "literal and symbolic marker"; *Pericles*, for example, mentions the six locales of the action—Tyre/Tyrus, Tharsus, Mytilene, Ephesus, Pentapolis, and Antioch—seventy-five times. Second, a comparison of the early play (with its many Christian allusions and several Italian names) to the later one reveals a greater effort by Shakespeare in *Pericles* to maintain historical and geographic coherence; such consistency can be seen in Pericles' travels, which reflect the navigational practices of ancient times, and in the political nomenclature that is more consistent with the reign of the Seleucid monarchs in the third and second centuries B.C.E. Third, the relatively benign view of the East (which McJannet finds) in these plays suggests a "paradoxical relation between humanist veneration for ancient Greek culture and Christian hostility to the Muslim Turks." Over time, the humanists' effort to assimilate the Hellenized East to their own moral universe may have contributed to the demonizing of infidels who, from the perspective of early modern Christians, had usurped the most revered sites of the ancient world. The cities alluded to in the two plays would have been known to Shakespeare's audiences, in part, through a supplement to later editions of Ortelius's *Theatrum Orbis Terrarum*, which included a map detailing places in the eastern Mediterranean visited by St. Paul.

Mowat, Barbara A. " 'I tell you what mine Authors saye': *Pericles*, Shakespeare, and *Imitatio*." *Archiv* 240 (2003): 42–59.

Mowat points out that the phrase "mine author" (or, to use its older variant, "mine auctor") had a "variety of resonances" in Shakespeare's time, most notably as (1) a source or literary authority, and (2) an authoritative writer whose work both served as a model for others and had become the subject of scholarly commentary. Gower's citation of his "authors" to introduce the story of father-daughter incest (1 Chor. 20) carries both meanings, thereby shifting the authority for the story "from the orally transmitted song to the written text" and, at the same time, transforming the representation of the narrator himself from the "singer of old songs to a scholar whose books and manuscripts provide him with the materials from which he draws." By thus citing the authority of its literary models, *Pericles* "announces its own constructedness and its rhetorical grounding in *imitatio*," a precept central to pedagogical and literary theory in early modern England. Mowat describes this pattern of construction as "an interweaving of material from two versions of the Apollonius story [Gower's *Confessio Amantis* and Twine's *The Patterne of Painefull Aduentures*] with elaborations from other traditions," along with Shakespearean innovations that sometimes echo his earlier plays and sometimes prefigure those yet to come. She singles out two scenes for special attention: the scene of Thaisa's death (3.1), which carries implications of the Mary Magdalene legend as disseminated in the *Golden Legend* and the *Digby Mary Magdalene* (a medieval saint's play); and the scene of Pericles' reunion with Marina (5.1), which includes among its authorities the tradition of Marian rhetoric and the *mater et filia* topos. As an exercise in *imitatio*, *Pericles* typifies the compositional practice Shakespeare uses throughout his career. Without question, he interweaves and transforms his authors so as to make what results his own creation, but "it is, at core, *imitatio* that is the ground of his invention, *imitatio* that he manipulates and transcends."

Mowat, Barbara A. " 'What's in a Name': Tragicomedy, Romance, or Late Comedy." In *A Companion to Shakespeare's Works*, edited by Richard Dutton and Jean Howard, 4:129–49. Malden, Mass.: Blackwell, 2004.

While it is a given in current Shakespeare studies that *Per.*, *Cym.*, *WT*, and *Temp.* belong to the same genre, there is less agreement about what the plays should be called. The cause of this "impasse," Mowat suggests, may arise "from problems inherent in the generic names themselves," especially the two most frequently used: *romance* and *tragicomedy*. Although it has proved the most "durable" (beginning with Dowden in the late nineteenth century), *romance* was not a recognizable category of Jacobean drama and even today seems more at home in the narrative form. The problem with *tragicomedy* is that Shakespeare's late dramas (despite shared features) appear different in kind from Fletcherian tragicomedy and the tragicomic vision of Guarini. Drawing on Wittgenstein's "theory of family resemblance," Mowat proposes an inherited generic DNA that renders both *romance* and *tragicomedy* "truly useful names for Shakespeare's late plays," in that both point to the family to which these plays belong. Her review of sixteenth-century dramatic romances from *Clyomon and Clamydes* through *Mucedorus* reveals a native (rather than Italianate) tradition of tragicomedy compatible with romance stories of journeys, loss, resonant family reunions, and improbable events. In their transformations of older forms, Shakespeare's "sophisticated 'mouldy tales' " may best be understood as "tragicomic romances."

Pitcher, John. "The Poet and the Taboo: The Riddle of Shakespeare's *Pericles*." *Essays and Studies* 35 (1982): 14–29.

Contesting the orthodox view that the first two acts of *Pericles* are negligible, Pitcher claims a continuity between the early and later acts that "is related to the danger, or *periculum* in Pericles himself." Behind what he concedes to be an unsophisticated development of the incest motif in Acts 1 and 2, Pitcher discerns an intelligence that shapes the narrative so as to "signal . . . the keynote of incest in Antioch, extrapolate . . . it in Tarsus, and leave . . . it provocatively unresolved in Pentapolis." No matter where Pericles travels, and whatever the precipitating cause of his adventures, the incestuous relationship "reassert[s] itself, in varied forms, until it is extirpated" in his marriage to Thaisa (2.5). But even as late as Act 4, the danger of incest remains in the purposeless drifting of the prince who, believing his daughter to be dead, may chance upon her in a brothel and consummate a sexual union, thereby locking the pattern begun in Antioch "into a tragic symmetry." Tragedy does not ensue because of the permutations *Pericles* works on what Northrop Frye calls the "comic Oedipus situation" at the heart of Menandrine New Comedy. Figured and refigured in the imagery of the early acts, the prolonged threat of an incestuous encounter in the later acts creates a "continuity of attention" to the theme of incest.

Relihan, Constance C. "Liminal Geography: *Pericles* and the Politics of Place." *Philological Quarterly* 71 (1992): 281–99. [Reprinted in *New Casebooks: Shakespeare's Romances*, edited by Alison Thorne, pp. 71–90. Basingstoke, England: Palgrave Macmillan, 2003.]

Attending to the "geopolitical implications of Shakespearean topography" in *Pericles*, Relihan examines the play's Greek, North African, and Aegean cultures as "liminal" sites, i.e., "thresholds connecting the European West and the Asiatic/African East." When taken with Pericles' own abdication of his political responsibilities, the dysfunctional governments found in the play's other locales reflect similar problems in the court of James I. In contrast to McJannet, Relihan finds in *Pericles* a hostile view of the Islamic East, which she attributes to the problems early modern Christians had in distinguishing between a past associated with classical Greek and New Testament traditions and a present connected with the threat posed by the infidel, non-European Ottoman empire. By using liminal locations and by emphasizing the drama's Otherness through the distancing mechanism of Gower's narrative control, Shakespeare "undermines interpretations of the play that see it affirming James I's reign and time's ability to heal and restore." To illustrate her critical rather than pro-Jamesian reading of the play, Relihan cites a 1581 tale by Barnaby Rich about a devil who assumes the shape of a gentleman, marries, flees London because of his wife's profligate spending, and goes on to inhabit the body of Scotland's James VI before ultimately returning to hell. When republished in 1606, in response to James's ascension to the English throne as James I, "the Turk" and "Constantinople" were substituted for references to "James" and "his court." Identifying Turks with the devil posed no cultural difficulties, and the easy substitution suggests an

unconscious sense in which both the infidel and the
king represent what is alien in English culture. The
sense of both 'us' and 'them' inherent in the liminal cultures of *Pericles* parallels "similar anxiety over the liminal nature of James I."

Skeele, David. *Thwarting the Wayward Seas: A Critical
and Theatrical History of Shakespeare's Pericles in the
Nineteenth and Twentieth Centuries*. Newark: University of Delaware Press; London: Associated University
Presses, 1998.

With an eye to both critics and directors, as well as
the cultural forces within which they operate, Skeele
chronicles the journey of *Pericles* from its vilification in
the nineteenth century to its "gradual acceptance and
even glorification" in the twentieth. Among the oft-
cited reasons given for the play's controversial status—
the question of authorship, the uneven quality of the
writing, the bawdy nature of much of the material, and
the choppy, episodic structure—Skeele singles out the
last. The play's fragmented structure—condemned in
the nineteenth century, denied by modern critics in
their quest to impose unity on the play, and reaffirmed
without censure by postmodern critics and directors—
serves as the "linchpin" of his study. Specific chapters
are titled *"Pericles* Meets the Victorian Critics," *"Pericles* on the Victorian Stage," "The Unified *Pericles*,"
"Simplicity and Unity," and *"Pericles* Deconstructed."

Skeele, David, ed. *Pericles: Critical Essays*. New York:
Garland, 2000.

The first part of this anthology (following an introduc-
tory overview of the scholarship and performance history related to *Pericles*) provides twenty-one critical
commentaries spanning the seventeenth through the
twentieth centuries; the second part is devoted to

accounts of theater productions between 1854 and 1994. Along with selected passages from Jonson ("Ode to Himself"), Lillo (his eighteenth-century adaptation *Marina*), early editors such as Malone and Steevens, and such nineteenth-century commentators as F. G. Fleay, W. W. Lloyd, George Brandes, and Swinburne, Skeele reprints excerpts from the following: G. Wilson Knight, *The Crown of Life* (1947); Howard Felperin, *Shakespearean Romance* (1972); C. L. Barber and Richard Wheeler, *The Whole Journey* (1986); Coppélia Kahn, "The Providential Tempest and the Shakespearean Family" (1980); Steven Mullaney, *The Place of the Stage: License, Play, and Power in Renaissance England* (1988); Janet Adelman, *Suffocating Mothers* (1991); and Skeele's critical and theatrical history annotated above. In addition to reprinted essays by Phyllis Gorfain ("Puzzle and Artifice: The Riddle as Metapoetry in *Pericles*," 1976) and J. R. Mulryne (" 'To glad your ear and please your eye': *Pericles* at the Other Place," 1979), the volume includes eight new essays: Marianne Novy, "Multiple Parenting in *Pericles*"; Lisa Hopkins, " 'The Shores of My Mortality': *Pericles'* Greece of the Mind"; Caroline Bicks, "Backsliding at Ephesus: Shakespeare's Diana and the Churching of Women"; Michael Baird Saenger, "*Pericles* and the Burlesque of Romance"; Thomas Rimer, "The Longest Voyage of All: Shakespeare's *Pericles* in Japan"; Melissa Gibson, "*Pericles* at the Royal National Theatre [1994]"; Paul Nelsen, "Shot from the Canon: The BBC Video of *Pericles*"; and Dale Moffitt, "*Pericles* and the Prospect Theatre." Samuel Phelps's 1854 *Pericles* at Sadler's Wells is the subject of two reviews and one essay; other productions reviewed include those of John Coleman (1900), Robert Atkins (1921), the Boston Shakespeare Company (1983), and the Hartford Stage Company (1987).

Womack, Peter. "Shakespeare and the Sea of Stories." *Journal of Medieval and Early Modern Studies* 29 (1999): 169–88.

An odd resemblance between the romance *Pericles* and the fifteenth-century miracle play *Mary Magdalen* is explained by tracing both to a common repertory of stories shared among ancient Greek romance and early mystery religions such as Christianity. These stories, according to Womack, were the real object of the attacks and defenses of the stage mounted in the sixteenth century by the likes of Stephen Gosson and Philip Sidney. Both sides of the debate sought to "decatholicize" the stage, either by banning theater altogether or by allowing dramatic illusion but not pseudo-miracle. *Pericles*, however, with its emphasis on storytelling and improbabilities of plot, and drawing heavily on miracle and withdrawal (gests typical of saints' legends), frustrates Sidneian theories of theater by harking back to pre-Reformation theater practices, a technique that prompted Jonson in turn to dismiss the play as a "mouldy tale." It is unnecessary to argue that *Pericles* is a cloaked Catholic play or to assume that Shakespeare had Catholic sympathies in order to understand how "a Catholic audience [could] reconnect with sacred drama just by the way it watched" this secular drama.

Shakespeare's Language

Abbott, E. A. *A Shakespearian Grammar.* New York: Haskell House, 1972.

This compact reference book, first published in 1870, helps with many difficulties in Shakespeare's language. It systematically accounts for a host of differences between Shakespeare's usage and sentence structure and our own.

Blake, Norman. *Shakespeare's Language: An Introduction.* New York: St. Martin's Press, 1983.
This general introduction to Elizabethan English discusses various aspects of the language of Shakespeare and his contemporaries, offering possible meanings for hundreds of ambiguous constructions.

Dobson, E. J. *English Pronunciation, 1500–1700.* 2 vols. Oxford: Clarendon Press, 1968.
This long and technical work includes chapters on spelling (and its reformation), phonetics, stressed vowels, and consonants in early modern English.

Houston, John. *Shakespearean Sentences: A Study in Style and Syntax.* Baton Rouge: Louisiana State University Press, 1988.
Houston studies Shakespeare's stylistic choices, considering matters such as sentence length and the relative positions of subject, verb, and direct object. Examining plays throughout the canon in a roughly chronological, developmental order, he analyzes how sentence structure is used in setting tone, in characterization, and for other dramatic purposes.

Onions, C. T. *A Shakespeare Glossary.* Oxford: Clarendon Press, 1986.
This revised edition updates Onions's standard, selective glossary of words and phrases in Shakespeare's plays that are now obsolete, archaic, or obscure.

Robinson, Randal. *Unlocking Shakespeare's Language: Help for the Teacher and Student.* Urbana, Ill.:

National Council of Teachers of English and the ERIC Clearinghouse on Reading and Communication Skills, 1989.

Specifically designed for the high-school and undergraduate college teacher and student, Robinson's book addresses the problems that most often hinder present-day readers of Shakespeare. Through work with his own students, Robinson found that many readers today are particularly puzzled by such stylistic devices as subject-verb inversion, interrupted structures, and compression. He shows how our own colloquial language contains comparable structures, and thus helps students recognize such structures when they find them in Shakespeare's plays. This book supplies worksheets—with examples from major plays—to illuminate and remedy such problems as unusual sequences of words and the separation of related parts of sentences.

Williams, Gordon. *A Dictionary of Sexual Language and Imagery in Shakespearean and Stuart Literature.* 3 vols. London: Athlone Press, 1994.

Williams provides a comprehensive list of the words to which Shakespeare, his contemporaries, and later Stuart writers gave sexual meanings. He supports his identification of these meanings by extensive quotations.

Shakespeare's Life

Baldwin, T. W. *William Shakspere's Petty School.* Urbana: University of Illinois Press, 1943.

Baldwin here investigates the theory and practice of the petty school, the first level of education in Elizabethan England. He focuses on that educational system primarily as it is reflected in Shakespeare's art.

Baldwin, T. W. *William Shakspere's Small Latine and Lesse Greeke*. 2 vols. Urbana: University of Illinois Press, 1944.

Baldwin attacks the view that Shakespeare was an uneducated genius—a view that had been dominant among Shakespeareans since the eighteenth century. Instead, Baldwin shows, the educational system of Shakespeare's time would have given the playwright a strong background in the classics, and there is much in the plays that shows how Shakespeare benefited from such an education.

Beier, A. L., and Roger Finlay, eds. *London 1500–1700: The Making of the Metropolis*. New York: Longman, 1986.

Focusing on the economic and social history of early modern London, these collected essays probe aspects of metropolitan life, including "Population and Disease," "Commerce and Manufacture," and "Society and Change."

Bentley, G. E. *Shakespeare's Life: A Biographical Handbook*. New Haven: Yale University Press, 1961.

This "just-the-facts" account presents the surviving documents of Shakespeare's life against an Elizabethan background.

Chambers, E. K. *William Shakespeare: A Study of Facts and Problems*. 2 vols. Oxford: Clarendon Press, 1930.

Analyzing in great detail the scant historical data, Chambers's complex, scholarly study considers the nature of the texts in which Shakespeare's work is preserved.

Cressy, David. *Education in Tudor and Stuart England*. London: Edward Arnold, 1975.

This volume collects sixteenth-, seventeenth-, and early-eighteenth-century documents detailing aspects of formal education in England, such as the curriculum, the control and organization of education, and the education of women.

Dutton, Richard. *William Shakespeare: A Literary Life.* New York: St. Martin's Press, 1989.
Not a biography in the traditional sense, Dutton's very readable work nevertheless "follows the contours of Shakespeare's life" as he examines Shakespeare's career as playwright and poet, with consideration of his patrons, theatrical associations, and audience.

Honan, Park. *Shakespeare: A Life.* New York: Oxford University Press, 1998.
Honan's accessible biography focuses on the various contexts of Shakespeare's life—physical, social, political, and cultural—to place the dramatist within a lucidly described world. The biography includes detailed examinations of, for example, Stratford schooling, theatrical politics of 1590s London, and the careers of Shakespeare's associates. The author draws on a wealth of established knowledge and on interesting new research into local records and documents; he also engages in speculation about, for example, the possibilities that Shakespeare was a tutor in a Catholic household in the north of England in the 1580s and that he played particular roles in his own plays, areas that reflect new, but unproven and debatable, data—though Honan is usually careful to note where a particular narrative "has not been capable of proof or disproof."

Schoenbaum, S. *William Shakespeare: A Compact Documentary Life.* New York: Oxford University Press, 1977.
This standard biography economically presents the essential documents from Shakespeare's time in an accessible narrative account of the playwright's life.

Shakespeare's Theater

Bentley, G. E. *The Profession of Player in Shakespeare's Time, 1590–1642*. Princeton: Princeton University Press, 1984.

Bentley readably sets forth a wealth of evidence about performance in Shakespeare's time, with special attention to the relations between player and company, and the business of casting, managing, and touring.

Berry, Herbert. *Shakespeare's Playhouses*. New York: AMS Press, 1987.

Berry's six essays collected here discuss (with illustrations) varying aspects of the four playhouses in which Shakespeare had a financial stake: the Theatre in Shoreditch, the Blackfriars, and the first and second Globe.

Cook, Ann Jennalie. *The Privileged Playgoers of Shakespeare's London*. Princeton: Princeton University Press, 1981.

Cook's work argues, on the basis of sociological, economic, and documentary evidence, that Shakespeare's audience—and the audience for English Renaissance drama generally—consisted mainly of the "privileged."

Greg, W. W. *Dramatic Documents from the Elizabethan Playhouses*. 2 vols. Oxford: Clarendon Press, 1931.

Greg itemizes and briefly describes many of the play manuscripts that survive from the period 1590 to around 1660, including, among other things, players' parts. His second volume offers facsimiles of selected manuscripts.

Gurr, Andrew. *Playgoing in Shakespeare's London*. 2nd ed. Cambridge: Cambridge University Press, 1996.

Gurr charts how the theatrical enterprise developed

from its modest beginnings in the late 1560s to become a thriving institution in the 1600s. He argues that there were important changes over the period 1567–1644 in the playhouses, the audience, and the plays.

Harbage, Alfred. *Shakespeare's Audience.* New York: Columbia University Press, 1941.
    Harbage investigates the fragmentary surviving evidence to interpret the size, composition, and behavior of Shakespeare's audience.

Hattaway, Michael. *Elizabethan Popular Theatre: Plays in Performance.* London: Routledge and Kegan Paul, 1982.
    Beginning with a study of the popular drama of the late Elizabethan age—a description of the stages, performance conditions, and acting of the period—this volume concludes with an analysis of five well-known plays of the 1590s, one of them (*Titus Andronicus*) by Shakespeare.

Shapiro, Michael. *Children of the Revels: The Boy Companies of Shakespeare's Time and Their Plays.* New York: Columbia University Press, 1977.
    Shapiro chronicles the history of the amateur and quasi-professional child companies that flourished in London at the end of Elizabeth's reign and the beginning of James's.

The Publication of Shakespeare's Plays

Blayney, Peter W. M. *The First Folio of Shakespeare.* Hanover, Md.: Folger, 1991.
    Blayney's accessible account of the printing and later life of the First Folio—an amply illustrated catalog to a 1991 Folger Shakespeare Library exhibition—analyzes

the mechanical production of the First Folio, describing how the Folio was made, by whom and for whom, how much it cost, and its ups and downs (or, rather, downs and ups) since its printing in 1623.

Hinman, Charlton. *The Norton Facsimile: The First Folio of Shakespeare.* 2nd ed. New York: W. W. Norton, 1996.
   This facsimile presents a photographic reproduction of an "ideal" copy of the First Folio of Shakespeare; Hinman attempts to represent each page in its most fully corrected state. The second edition includes an important new introduction by Peter W. M. Blayney.

Hinman, Charlton. *The Printing and Proof-Reading of the First Folio of Shakespeare.* 2 vols. Oxford: Clarendon Press, 1963.
   In the most arduous study of a single book ever undertaken, Hinman attempts to reconstruct how the Shakespeare First Folio of 1623 was set into type and run off the press, sheet by sheet. He also provides almost all the known variations in readings from copy to copy.

Key to Famous Lines
and Phrases

The blind mole casts
Copped hills towards heaven, to tell the earth is
  thronged
By man's oppression, and the poor worm doth die for 't.
[*Pericles*—1.1.103–7]

The sad companion dull-eyed Melancholy.
[*Pericles*—1.2.3]

. . . the great ones [fish] eat up the little ones.
[*First Fisherman*—2.1.29–30]

A man whom both the waters and the wind
In that vast tennis court hath made the ball
For them to play upon entreats you pity him.
[*Pericles*—2.1.61–63]

Here's a fish hangs in the net like a poor man's right in
the law.
[*Second Fisherman*—2.1.121–22]

. . . thou dost look
Like Patience gazing on kings' graves and smiling
Extremity out of act.
[*Pericles*—5.1.157–59]

Thou that beget'st him that did thee beget.
[*Pericles*—5.1.229]